EAST
OF THE
CHESAPEAKE

EAST
OF THE
CHESAPEAKE

William H. Turner

Illustrations by the author

With a foreword by Tom Horton

The Johns Hopkins University Press

Baltimore and London

Dedicated to the memory of
Captain Clayton Frank Cisar, USMS
September 23, 1936–October 27, 1991
A friend in all weathers.

Copyright © William H. Turner, 1998
Originally published in hardcover by Turner Press in 1998
Printed in the United States of America on acid-free paper

Johns Hopkins Paperbacks edition, 2000
2 4 6 8 9 7 5 3 1

The Johns Hopkins University Press
2715 North Charles Street
Baltimore, Maryland 21218-4363
www.press.jhu.edu

Library of Congress Cataloging-in-Publication Data

Turner, William H. (William Henry), 1935–
East of the Chesapeake / William H. Turner ; illustrations by the
author ; with a foreword by Tom Horton.—Johns Hopkins pbk. ed.
p.   cm.
"Originally published in hardcover by Turner Press in 1998"—T.p. verso.
ISBN 0-8018-6470-4 (alk. paper)
1. Turner, William H. (William Henry), 1935—Childhood and youth.
2. Farm life—Chesapeake Bay Region (Md. and Va.) 3. Farm life—
Eastern Shore (Md. and Va.) 4. Chesapeake Bay Region (Md. and Va.)—
Biography. 5. Eastern Shore (Md. and Va.)—Biography. I. Title.

CT275.T955 A3 2000
975.5′18—dc21
99-059258

A catalog record for this book is available from the British Library.

CONTENTS

FOREWORD

There are two words these writings of Bill Turner's bring to mind—*insular*; also, *mundane*. Please don't mistake that for anything but praise.

The modern mind, and some dictionaries, have downgraded both terms, assigning to the former connotations of narrowness and standoffishness; and to the latter, intimations of the ordinary, the trivial and the boring.

But those are failings of the moderns mind, of a consciousness oriented more to Interstate highways than the marshy meanders of tidewater; to thinking that because a straight line is the fastest way to get somewhere, it is also the best.

In the world as recalled herein by Turner, *insular*—and its close cousin, *peninsular*—mean quite simply, from the Latin, lands bordered abundantly by water.

The intimate mingling of land with tidewater is the essential nature of Chesapeake Bay, which is some 200 miles long, yet enjoys a total shoreline of around 8,000 miles. And nowhere in the Bay region does this happy circumstance prevail more than on Virginia's Eastern Shore, the canvas for Turner's portraits of a boyhood admirably misspent.

His hometown dangles like the tail of a shrimp, between Atlantic and Chesapeake, from the bulkier peninsula of Delmarva. It is islanded from the rest of Virginia by Maryland on the north, and Chesapeake Bay to the west and south. Creeks and guts and rivers and inlets incise it deeply from both seaside and bayside, subdividing the land into an endless profusion of smaller insulae and peninsulae.

Ecologists think of all this shoreline as a type of "edge habitat," where the overlap of differing natural systems fosters a sort of hybrid vigor, life in extraordinary abundance and diversity. Hunters who walk the seams between forest and field, and fishermen progging the marshes and eelgrass beds knew this before there were ecologists.

But there is more to it than fish and game. I believe, and Turner's writings prove it, that the intricate braiding of land and water breeds more than ducks and rockfish. It breeds a specialness in the human spirit.

It has something to do with living, insulated by water down those long, skinny "necks," along dirt roads that just end where the dry land plays out. Just as peninsulas like Delmarva funnel migrations of warblers, monarch butterflies and peregrine falcons that collect at their tips before crossing the Bay's mouth, they also collect and distill generations of human experience.

As a result, places like the Eastern Shore of Virginia are filthy rich in characters, a wealth that will never show up on anyone's economic analysis.

This brings me to *mundane* which means, from the Latin, merely the world, nothing more, nothing less. Turner writes of fried blackbirds, of old slaves, of the seasons of the potato—white ones, sweet ones, and Haymans, a savory blend of both.

He speaks from experience, else how would he know that weed seed is superior to corn for baiting ducks, because it is less visible from the game warden's plane. Nor would a dilettante understand the virtues of an old Studebaker for night-shooting rabbits—better fenders were never made for straddling the headlight as you bumped through fields.

In pieces like *The Old Yellow House*, one of the finer vignettes of Shore life I have seen, he reflects on those "delicacies in season," like shad roe scrambled with gull eggs, strawberries and soft crabs, and recognizes what we have lost as we have gained modern refrigeration and shipping: ". . . subsistance farming provided certain delicacies at specific times and gave one something to miss and something to anticipate—two of the most soul-satisfying emotions of man."

All very earthly, very mundane if you will. And all, seived through the meshes of the author's memory, very full of that wonder of the everyday world, a wonder that Kenneth Grahame in *The Wind in the Willows* called "the most priceless possession of the human race."

The unexamined life, it has been said, is not a life worth living; nor is the unexamined place worth living in, I would add. By such a measure, *East of the Chesapeake* significantly enhances property values on the insular, mundane Virginia Shore that is its subject.

Tom Horton, author of
Bay Country, Waters Way,
Turning the Tide, Swanfall,
Island Out of Time, et al.

ix

PROLOGUE

Geography is a great shaper of personalities, from the humble and trifling to the famous and infamous. And while I will leave it to others to rank me on this comprehensive scale, I have always been amazed at the astronomical odds concerning my birthplace and constantly feel its moulding.

First, the Earth is, in my opinion and knowledge, one of the prime planets. And few will dispute the fact that North America is the prime continent. To make a comparison of the United States of America with Canada or Mexico is, of course, a needless waste of time. Everyone knows that Virginia, the birthplace of Washington and Jefferson, is certainly the foremost state in the nation. Here, one has a choice of mountains or coast, and nothing surpasses salt water for an environment. Then there is the narrow Virginian peninsula, which forms the southern and most important part of the Chesapeake Bay, the world's most beautiful estuary. This peninsula is surrounded by the Atlantic Ocean on the east and the Bay on the west. This is Virginia's Eastern Shore. It was here that I was destined to be born. Statistically, it is almost inconceivable that I was allowed to begin my life in this area. But by chance or design (I prefer the latter) I was so privileged, and I have always felt a certain degree of superiority over those who haven't had this opportunity.

This is a part of the answer to the question that many people ask me: "How and why did you become a sculptor?" And now many also ask me, "How and why did you became a writer?" As I try to point out at times in this book, life is a game of chance. The earlier in life one is affected by one of the infinitesimal number of chances, which will always pummel us like a hailstorm, the more profound will be the final result. When one is young and impressionable and when there are many paths ahead to trod, these pushes and pulls can have a distinct effect on one's final destination.

When I was a child, and becoming aware of my being and my environment, I noticed in the rear view mirror of the family truck that I had a blemish—a mole on my upper lip, half-way between the filtrum and the corner of my mouth. It was chocolate brown in color, about the diameter of the head of a tenpenny nail and slightly raised. Being aware of symmetry in myself and others (with the exception of the part in my hair), I suspected something was amiss. However, it did not concern me until my playmates began to try to pick it off. Their curiosity turned to ridicule. Just as a chicken with a deformity is singled out by its brethren for persecution, so was I. The teasing and mocking I received was relentless. Some said I had a dog tick fastened to my lip, and some said this "beauty mark" made me ugly. (I had it removed when I was fifteen and many still considered me ugly.)

Thus I became very sensitive and always tried to keep my left profile in view. This can be downright inconvenient if you are playing ring around the roses, hopscotch or wrestling. As a result I began to spend more and more time with my goat, my dog, my cat and my duck, as well as older people and some less particular friends who seemed to like me regardless of this cruel trick played on me by the gods. Also I spent a lot of time reading and drawing pictures. In short, I was inclined to entertain myself in ways that did not require a human companion, and the outdoors, with its opportunities to hunt, fish and trap, was always a safe haven.

Of course, this analyzing can go on and on with refinements and positive and negative influences until one has as complete an answer as possible to this very complex question. The resulting effect on me was that I became, to a certain degree, an introvert, just the kind of personality that lends itself to sculpture, painting and writing.

I suppose many books are reflections of the authors' minds. In this writing, there is little chronological order and much fragmentation. The truth is that my attention span, coupled with my sparse repertoire of knowledge and lack of imagination, will not allow me to write a novel or a history. I have simply recorded a few events, rumors and memories while there is time.

There are no really big words in this book. I know a few, and I'm sure most of my readers know a few. But unless we know the same ones this could be a problem and one would continuously reach for a dictionary. I dislike doing this and assume that my readers feel the same way.

I brought my last book to a conclusion knowing there was more to tell. However, I had to stop somewhere, publish, and begin again. It could have been three little books, two medium books, or perhaps I should have waited and published one big book, because in many ways the content of this one is more of the same. The satisfaction of seeing my thoughts in print, hopefully disseminated to thousands of readers, and not knowing what would happen to the manuscript if I were to prematurely perish, all influenced me to publish. It is like picking out crab meat; you pick it out and pile it up until you have a savory mouthful, and then you eat it. Then you pick and pile up some more. This is my second pile.

Some of these stories are as true as a block of granite. Others are fragments of rumors and memories mortared together in an artificial way, which I hope is entertaining, offers an insight into a bygone era, and above all sends a message that is probably not essential to one's continuation of life. The reader can tell which is which unless I am a better writer than I thought.

In some of the stories I have portrayed myself in a way that may lead one to believe I was neglected in my youth. This is not so. I was fortunate to have hardworking, responsible parents who looked after my sister and me in such a manner that we lacked for nothing of importance. I regret they did not live to see my work published.

ACKNOWLEDGMENTS

Working alone, I have built many craft and they all have floated. However, in building this one, Robert Hutchinson helped on the fastenings, Catherine Roberts did the fairing and William Nicholson caulked the seams. Finally, Nancy Irvin, who taught many of us, tuned the rig. Thus, I think it will sail a little better.

Unwittingly, my friends of the tower* helped. They talked and I ate my bacon and eggs and listened. They are Melvin, Webby, Johnny, Dave, Franky and Bagley. And there was Joe, who is gone.

---

*   Just as the mockingbird sits on the back of your lawn chair and enjoys the advantages of height, so is man inclined.

Although I do not know exactly when, there was a time when a human climbed upon a rock, tree or ant hill to have a better vantage of his terrain. From a height he was a more efficient predator and a less vulnerable prey. In the primordial wilderness, these two concerns were always paramount.

Gradually, as man's mind developed, he found that he could create structures in places of his own choosing that satisfied these demands of nature. These structures became more elaborate and eventually served another purpose—a place to think and observe, especially if what you see is yours.

Thus in 1996 I built a 16' x 16' observation room on 40' poles on the shores of the Chesapeake, where I can see most of my childhood playground and where much of this book was written.

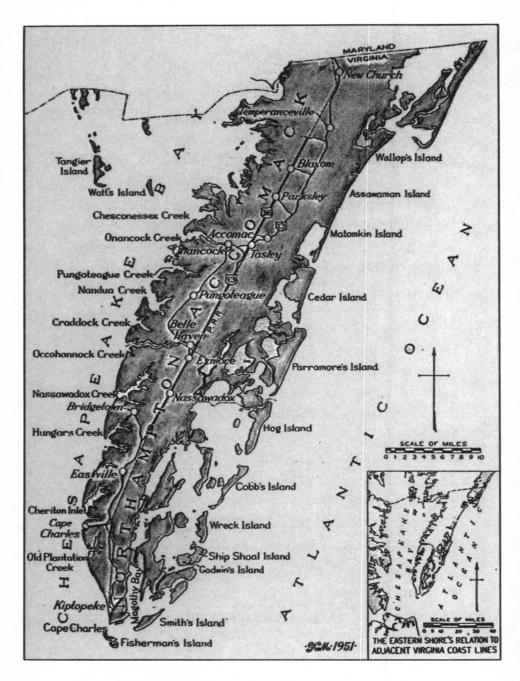

Taken from <u>Virginia's Eastern Shore</u> by Ralph T. Whitelaw. Courtesy of Picton Press.

That portion [of the Eastern Shore] at present included within the limits of Virginia is about seventy miles in length, extending from the Pocomoke River, near where it is intersected by the thirty-eighth parallel of north latitude, to Cape Charles, and having a mean breadth of about eight miles. It is a flat and sandy tract, largely covered with pines and swept by breezes of the Atlantic and Chesapeake, whose waters lave it on either side. The monotony of the country, due to the absence of mountains, hills or broken surface, is relieved by the picturesque bays and creeks which make up into the mainland at frequent intervals along its coasts.

Jennings Cropper Wise,
The Early History of the Eastern Shore of Virginia: Ye Kingdome of Accawmacke or the Eastern Shore of Virginia in the Seventeenth Century

Courtesy of Clearfield Co., Inc.

THE PATH

*So it was here in this peninsular Eden east of the Chesapeake, as the
Bay was named thousands of years ago, that a different mentality
of man was allowed to germinate . . .*

A thousand years ago or perhaps ten thousand, it makes
no difference, a whitetail deer browsed leisurely through the
virgin forest of what is now Virginia's Eastern Shore.
Evicted from his birthplace by a stronger buck, he sought
territory of his own. He ambled, in no particular direction,
drawn and repelled by negative or positive influences, a
phenomenon that affects all creatures at all times. He
deviated around a loblolly pine recently felled by a
hurricane, then darted ahead for several hundred yards when
a twig snapped within his radius of tolerance. This
relentless search for food, and an equally important instinct
to avoid becoming food, would determine every step of his
life.

In his travels, he encountered a thicket of blackberry
bushes. The blackberry thicket grew there because a
century before a bolt of lightning ignited a fire, which
destroyed part of the forest. The absence of a canopy

1

emitted light on the dung of a raccoon that had eaten blackberries on the banks of Occohannock Creek the day before. These seeds germinated, and the vines quickly spread into the rich, exposed topsoil, establishing their own impenetrable territory. Chance and opportunity are the way of nature's flora, as well as her fauna.

After browsing his way around the perimeter of this obstacle, the deer continued his trek. In the recesses of his primitive mind was a subconscious urge to head easterly to obtain salt from the ocean, where the ebb and flow of the tide had created residual pools that evaporated time and time again, creating a deliciously saline mud, attractive to many species. His sensitive nose received increasingly strong signals from this basic life-supporting substance, and his pace quickened.

He skirted around a large bog, the result of the earth's being scoured slightly deeper in this area during the last and recent ice age. The sound of the surf upon his sensitive ears told him he was nearing his goal. The loblolly pines eventually gave way to cedar and bayberry, then to a wide expanse of spartina grass dotted with saltwater ponds. Having satiated his body's demand for salt, he rested, and the following day returned along the same path, subconsciously mapping his route and remembering his reward.

On another occasion, this same deer trod upon this now subtly familiar track accompanied by a few others. As a result of repeated prints of sharp hooves, a trail began to be inscribed in the pristine wilderness, and generations of deer and lesser mammals followed this path of least resistance.

Eons later, a native American, pushed eastward by the expansion and aggression of fellow humans, came upon this path. He, too, was seeking food, and this game track held promise. He returned periodically because of its familiarity and the quietness it imparted to his constant stalking. Later his family and comrades came to use this same path, a convenient route to the seaside salt and  an easy way to move from Bay to sea as the seasons suggested.

Somewhere to the south of this meandering but generally east-west path across the long and narrow peninsula that forms the Chesapeake Bay, a party of these primitive hunters encountered a huge wooly mammoth with her newborn calf. The offspring was easily killed and attention was turned to the adult. Despite her wounds, she fled—creating a path through briars and bushes that were no obstacle to such a huge creature. In her fight to escape, the beast crossed the old east-west path and continued northward in a frantic effort to survive. Eventually, after hours of being speared and clubbed, the life and blood ebbed from her huge, beautiful body, which would now nourish her Stone Age executioners. And as a result of this bounty, one more infant would survive to become a hunter and it, too, would have a child.

It was winter, a good time for a protein windfall such as this. The mammoth's flesh and that of her calf would support the extended family of about thirty until spring, when fish would be abundant and shellfish easier to harvest. Many trips were made back and forth from one carcass to another, following the path the doomed, lumbering beast had created as it trampled the vegetation. Thus a narrow, but clear and permanent north-south route was quickly established, which would always remain and ultimately affect modern man.

On leaving their bark huts and coming to this intersection, the local population was able to travel in other general directions with relative ease. They came to use this same path for various reasons, usually looking for food, but occasionally visiting relatives or friends or participating in festivities, if the whims of nature allowed such extravagances.

As the aboriginal population slowly mastered its environment and increased over the centuries, chance encounters along the paths became more frequent. The intersection of these paths became a convenient place to leave crude messages to neighbors with shells and sticks. Knowing that friends, relatives or perhaps enemies would later or sooner cross this intersection made it a favorite waiting place.

One afternoon, a group returning from the ocean side with a reed basket full of oysters and armfuls of meat from a whale beached in the surf encountered at this place another group that had killed a deer. A partial exchange of commodities ensued, and the groups agreed to meet at this point again on the first day following the next full moon.

So it was that an almost imperceptible trading of commodities began. Eventually these exchanges would become routine and lead to specialization, and thus increased efficiency. To divide and conquer became man's unconscious strategy against nature. With more productivity came more free time and energy and thus more children, and the population continued to grow.

Exchanges at the intersection became a part of the culture of these innocent children of the forest, and eventually it was decided to fell the trees in this area. The resulting hiatus in the verdant umbrella of pines would allow the rays of sun to bring warmth and light to the incipient coagulation of humanity below. The huge trees were killed with a fire at their roots, as a witch would be burned at the stake, and the fallen trunks became wayside benches for weary travelers or those who were waiting to trade.

This immediate area, therefore, took on an altered look as the human presence pushed back the forest and held it at bay. It was a good place to be if you were lonely, hungry or had something to trade.

This slight inclination toward specialization brought about by increase in trade, permitted and encouraged by the primitive crossroads, increased over the millennia. This is the way of nature; changes in the behavior of any species have repercussions—sometimes good, sometimes bad, but usually a combination of both.

So it was here in this peninsular Eden east of the Chesapeake, as the Bay was named thousands of years ago, that a different mentality of man was allowed to germinate and eventually prosper.

You see, there was a time when you were either killed or allowed to starve, depending upon the philosophy of your people, if you could not catch fish in the summer and kill deer in the winter. If you were not proficient at these things, and hundreds more, you were not allowed to live at the expense of your fellow humans.

As trade and travel increased, opportunities emerged and a young man of the western tribe who was inherently lazy was sent to the intersection with a deer carcass belonging to his family to trade for some pumpkins from the people of the south, knowing that they also traveled these paths. He did this satisfactorily and was allowed a few morsels of pumpkin and venison. His attendance at this crossroads meant that his fellow humans, who were stronger and more efficient hunters and gatherers, did not have to waste time in waiting if the shells and sticks were misinterpreted, if the sun's position was not accurately judged, or if clouds obscured the moon.

This indolent young man was pleased with this arrangement, because it filled his belly and he was allowed to live. With time, he decided to build a hut at this location and also make exchanges for the people of the north and the people of the east. It was agreed by all of the tribes that he would be allowed to take his living from the labor of others. In time, he became more than the guardian of other people's produce and began to be mediator or broker and to put himself in the position of telling others what to bring to him. Soon he began to demand a share of the exchange that exceeded his needs, while others went hungry. And so his wealth accumulated, and he burned down a few more trees and employed someone to help him in his occupation, which gradually took on aspects of extortion, manipulation, price fixing and usury. It is true that all these traits did not mature completely in one generation, but they did begin to develop, and we experience the results today.

Thus, these paths and their crossing became a vital part of the small world of these aboriginal inhabitants. They grew more delineated as time passed, but never became wider than the space needed for a single file of humans, except around the crowded intersection, which was now permeated with a miasma of the human presence.

No one knows for certain where this sure and slow change in the culture would have led. It was as unpredictable as the path made by the evicted buck somewhere in the distant past. There were people of another world on this planet, however, and the end of this natural way of life was just around the bend.

Although these paths and the forest they penetrated had been the home of other humans for thousands of years when the first Europeans arrived, the King across the ocean granted to a minor but allegiant official a huge tract of the beautiful land he had never seen. The Indians were exterminated either by disease or the sword, and perhaps the latter was more merciful.

Eventually this bureaucrat sold a parcel of the land grant for a wagonload of salt. The "Indian paths," as they were now called, were convenient boundaries. Trees were cleared close to the path and newcomers built small cabins. This was repeated on each side of the path, which had been widened so an ox cart could pass, and a trading post was built at the crossing. The white man knew as well as the yellow man that where paths intersect one finds the most people. The meanderings extending beyond this point were retained to define the property lines long before there were surveyors.

The owner of this huge block of stolen earth, bordered by the ocean and the Bay and the path Nature's creatures had marked out eons ago, had reason to further divide this land because he had offspring who needed territory as did the bear, the wolf and the deer. In the absence of a sufficient natural boundary, he went through the woods of 400-year-old loblolly pines with circumferences of 15 to 18 feet and blazed the ancient trees with an axe. And so the land became raped and divided, and people increased. The virgin forest was cleared and became fields. In those days, the magnificent trees were considered a nuisance that needed to be destroyed to allow rays of sun to reach tobacco and corn. But the meanderings of the paths did not change.

As those children grew and established families, the

8

land was divided again and again. The boundaries were sometimes man's sterile, straight lines on paper and earth and sometimes nature's waterways, large and small, and the paths. As traffic increased, the paths became rough roads and the day came when the first motor vehicle crept laboriously along the ruts that followed the Indian path, which followed the game trail determined by the whims of the unknown whitetail buck centuries ago.

In a few years there were more of these machines and the paths were widened to accommodate their size and numbers. The owners along each side gave up a little land, which was still plentiful, and the ancient paths became highways.

That is why the roads meander and how Kmart came to be at the intersection of Mammoth Boulevard and Salt Lick Avenue. And it all began when the mammoth cow ran north across the old Indian trail a long time ago when the planet was a nicer place to be.

LIZZIE BIBBINS AND MY HAT

. . . "I am of the Cherokee nation."

That spring and summer I helped my grandmother cut turnip greens for the table from the field edges where they grew wild. These plants sent up tall spikes that developed into yellow flowers. I thought they made a pleasing arrangement when combined with the blues and purples of the wild violets and bell flowers, the reds of the cardinal flowers and the yellows of the dandelions, which we picked for their beauty. She also had a very "snaky" garden of domestic flowers adjacent to her house, which was lush and overgrown. One could not see the ground because of ivy and other vines. To wind through this floral maze was like penetrating the Amazon rain forest—not knowing what to expect under the foliage or around the corner.

It should be noted that I was also interested in frogs, slingshots, minnows and other such genderly more appropriate items of my rural environment. I loved to help my grandfather make barrels for his potatoes or watch him make shoes for his mules.

But I enjoyed tagging along behind my grandmother as well as my grandfather—it did me no harm and it was she who kindled my interest in botany. She pointed out that all these beautiful flowers would produce seeds later in the year. To prove her point, or perhaps more appropriately to teach me, we returned in the fall to see these plants' stepping stones into the future.

My mother, always a very industrious person, told me that I could sell the turnip green seeds, so I set about collecting them. I gathered a potato sack full of the long thin pods, but the seeds had to be separated from the chaff, so she taught me how to winnow them. After beating the bag with a stick, the contents were spread out on a bed sheet on a windy day and tossed into the air over and over and, as one probably knows from reading the Bible, the seeds were eventually lying alone on the sheet. I did this on many occasions until I had about fifteen pounds of these very fine capsules of nucleic acid. My goal was to earn enough money to buy a straw cowboy hat from the dime store in Exmore, the nearest town. We went to this metropolis of about three hundred people once a week to shop for staples and sometimes to see a movie. We always purchased our groceries from James' Market and sometimes bartered with eggs. They graciously purchased my seeds for $1.50, and I used this money to buy my hat from the store across the street, which was U.S. 13, the Ocean Highway.

It is interesting how an object of significance when paired with an event links the two in a lasting complementary manner, and conjuring up one always brings along the other no matter how, when, or which comes first. Of course, this hat was not important beyond its time, and this Saturday evening in town was no different from any of the others except that it was on the return from this particular trip that I first saw Lizzie Bibbins.

The trip of about eight miles along a dirt road, which led to our home at the bottom of Occohannock Neck, took on a different aspect that night, and things happened that became permanently imprinted in my mind and forever linked to my new hat. The moon was so full and so bright that my father did not need to put on the headlight (one was broken) of the truck. Normally, I would have fallen asleep in my mother's arms, but I took an interest in this reckless nighttime driving and enjoyed the eeriness of it all. We had not gone far, however, when the moon was suddenly obscured by a black cloud and we were enveloped by a blizzard accompanied by thunder and lightning. My parents commented to themselves about this strange meteorological phenomenon, and even though I was only four or five years old, their puzzlement was contagious.

My father turned on the headlight, and we crept along at a pace no greater than the top speed of my tricycle. The snowflakes looked as big as baseballs, and they seemed to be coming directly at us, almost horizontally, as a barrage of tracer bullets.

My father was concerned about the gas supply because of the headwind and was leaning over the steering wheel with his face as close to the cracked windshield as possible, as if to urge the family vehicle onward. I was enjoying the adventure when I felt the braking of the truck. Looking over the hood, my eyes fell upon an apparition close to the fender, and for the first time in my life I saw Lizzie Bibbins.

She stood in the road glaring back at us in a daring manner. Her clothes, which appeared to be a series of calico blankets, were flapping in the breeze like a luffing sail, and she had an immense sack on her back decorated with strange symbols. At this point, it was difficult to see her face, but as my father rode cautiously ahead, my mother rolled down her window and asked this specter-like person if she desired a ride. As she looked down into the cab carefully scrutinizing each of us, one by one, in a systematic foot-to-head manner, it became apparent that this was a middle-aged woman of extreme height. This was certainly not a unilateral visual exercise, and I think all three of us were surely looking at her, and my parents were looking at each other as well. Her voice was neither black nor white, male nor female, and it could not be described with any relevance to anyone we had heard except perhaps over the radio. For our neck of the woods, it was different—but still precise and almost elegant—I guess that's what made the difference. I'll never forget her reply, "I don't ride with strange people," and she turned her back to us and continued on into the blinding snow. My mother was rebuffed on her second invitation to ride, and we continued on. Neither of my parents had ever seen this person before, and from their remarks I don't think that they were looking forward to another encounter.

Holding on to my new hat, trying to figure it all out, I queried my mother about what or who that was but, as I recall, I received no definitive answer.

Soon we arrived home, and after the wood heater was stoked we sat around and enjoyed the radiating warmth and some crisp gingersnaps and rat cheese. My parents discussed the events of the evening, especially the strange storm. We did not know it at the time, but this was just the beginning of about three years of an unusual kind of weather that would be detrimental to the already depression-troubled local economy. That entire winter was a prolonged freeze-up that affected the harvest of oysters. The following spring was too wet and the summer was too dry for the farmers. Violent nor'westers kept the rum-runners in port much of the time, and their business suffered. Then came a series of hurricanes that seemed to zero in on the Chesapeake Bay area. One did not know they were coming and did not know when they would abate—especially frightening for a child.

Not long after my first encounter with this strange person (it was later that I learned her name was Lizzie Bibbins), I experienced some remarkably good fortune and found a soda bottle in the ditch in front of our house. I immediately took this to Mr. Stewart's store to trade for a penny piece of candy. When I entered the store, no one was there except the owner. My nose was pressed against the glass candy case, mulling over the choices, and I realized that the proprietor was getting a little impatient waiting for the consummation of this sale. The door of the store opened, and, although I heard this, I did not look around until a nearby board squeaked. Turning around, my eyes first encountered a calico blanket draped over a figure. I tilted my head back almost vertically and observed Lizzie's strange face. First, I noticed that she wore gold earrings, whose weight had, over the years, enlarged the holes in her lobes to something less than snug. The metal blended with the bronze color of her skin, and I couldn't make up my mind if she were the darkest white person or the lightest black person I had ever seen. She seemed to realize my dilemma and looked down at me with brown eyes that sparkled with amusement at my amazement and asked, "Do you think I'm black or white?" Then seeing my inability to speak, she said proudly, "I am of the Cherokee nation."

I was relieved when her attention shifted to Mr. Stewart and she purchased some pipe tobacco that came in the red and green Prince Albert tin containers. Before leaving, however, she again focused her attention on me. "I've seen that hat before," she said as she gently lifted it a few inches off my head. Her next words were the last I ever heard from her, "That pretty blonde hair would make a nice scalp." And then she quietly left after putting her purchases into that same strangely lettered cloth sack.

"Only fools and children tell their dreams," an old sage once told me, and I have, over the years, made that one of my cardinal rules, so I won't tell you about my dream that night. I can say, however, that I believe it was the first dream I ever remembered, and it is still vivid whenever I choose to recall it.

This apparition did not appear before me again that winter, and my next sighting was in the spring, when white potatoes were being dug on my grandfather Turner's farm. Playing around with some children of the field hands in the newly plowed earth, it dawned upon me that it was beginning to get dark. I looked at the unopened brown paper bag containing the lunch my grandmother had packed for me and rationalized that this darkness was untimely. Such is the logic of childhood. The air grew cooler and the birds stopped singing. The field hands stopped scratching potatoes from the earth and pointed to the disappearing sun; I was experiencing my first eclipse. Anxiety was evident among some of the adults, and it created an uneasy feeling with my playmates and me. To add to the feelings of insecurity, Lizzie Bibbins suddenly walked out of the woods and across the potato field. The laborers parted in front of her as Central Park pigeons do for a pedestrian, and she soon disappeared into the woods on the opposite side of the field with all eyes upon her.

Her voice had reached my ears twice, and I had now seen her three times. I was never to see her again because my parents soon gave up life on the farm and we reluctantly moved into town. The future would be ripe with rumors, but that's all the direct contact that I ever had with Ms. Bibbins, and at that age it was all I wanted, plus a little. Of course, as I write this, I would pay dearly for an interview.

No one knew where she lived, and she was seldom seen. But my Aunt Zode recalled years later, after people had begun to put things together as much as they dared, the time Lizzie came to her house to borrow sugar. Aunt Zode's robust young son, Haywood, had been playing on the front porch when Lizzie approached. He ran into the house to tell his mother, who came to the door. Lizzie said she wished to borrow sugar, but Aunt Zode didn't have any. Now this was true because a lot of things were in short supply in those times and besides, Aunt Zode, being a devout Christian, would never lie. However, Lizzie did not believe her and left in an agitated state mumbling in indiscernible tongues. This incident was quickly forgotten by Aunt Zode, and soon she had other things on her mind more important than worrying about being on the outs with this tall yellow woman. A few days later Haywood began to feel sickly. All sorts of remedies were administered such as kerosene and molasses, mustard plasters and castor oil. The local doctor was consulted, and he could not find any medical reason for the child's illness. Eventually Aunt Zode took her son to Norfolk so the specialists could see him, but nothing helped and the child slowly grew more frail.

Later that fall, Aunt Zode was raking leaves from under her front porch when she came upon a sock with a knot tied in the opening. Inside were nine bent pins, some feathers, plaited grass and a lump of a white substance. She threw the whole thing into the leaf pile, burned it and forgot it. It was a puzzling thing, but she had work to do and had to care for a sick son.

In only a few days, events took a turn for the better and Haywood began to recover. In a couple of weeks he was back to normal and returned to school.

There was another occasion the following spring when a sock full of nonsense objects was found in Red Kilmon's boat. Red had pulled his boat up to scrape off the barnacles and to paint it, thinking this might change his luck. He had been having a poor year catching fish in his pound-nets while his competitors were doing fine. While cleaning out the boat, he found the sock, which was hidden under some rope under the bow. As he related years later when the speculation began, it was just an ordinary wool sock, but in it were some bent pins, gull feathers, plaited grass, rope and fish scales. He threw it overboard along with the rest of his trash and paint scrapings, allowing the ebb tide to take it away. He put his boat in the water, and from then on caught plenty of fish.

It was only years later, when Red was retired, sitting on his front porch rocking and thinking about all the wonderful people who had happily bought his fish during his long career, that he recalled his problem with Lizzie Bibbins. It seems that one day she walked out of the woods on the Custis farm while Red was coming down the road blowing his fish horn. Lizzie stopped him and bought a big croaker. The following day she appeared again in the same spot and wanted another fish claiming the first one was rotten. Well, of course, he knew that all of his fish were fresh with black eyes and red gills, but he gave her another one anyway.

This did not please Lizzie. She thought it was a trifle smaller than the first one and returned to the woods, cursing.

No one else seemed to have any problem with Lizzie, and she kept pretty much to herself. At times she would be seen gleaning the fields in the distance or walking the road late at night, always with her strangely marked sack.

In the meantime, the economy suffered, mainly because of the weather. Some people were thinking of moving just as the folks did in *Grapes of Wrath*, but they did not know where to go. They were hemmed in by the Ocean on the east and the Bay on the west, and certainly no one would head north!

Eventually, people realized that Lizzie had disappeared. No one cared much one way or another, because she never really caused any obvious trouble and kept to herself somewhere out in the woods. What everyone began to think about was the change in the weather. It seemed to rain when corn was tasseling and needed it and stayed dry and sunny in the fall when the crop was being harvested. The oystermen weren't frozen out so much and the rum runners weren't getting blown about at night by the nor'westers as they had been in the past few years.

In those days, in a good Christian community such as ours, people were always thankful if no one starved and the sun kept coming up. No one would ever openly speculate about an extraneous supernatural force—that would have been blasphemy.

Of course, I am also conservative, but I will relate

another incident, not implying there is any connection. It had been about ten years since Lizzie was last seen when an interesting discovery was made in a defunct moonshiner's shanty deep in the woods on the old Custis farm. I don't think the position is open today or else I would apply for it—but the state at one time employed a person referred to as "revenooer" by the local people, to search the woods looking for moonshiners. John Mapp held this position for years, and he worked very hard roaming the woods and fields. He enjoyed his work but always had his shotgun and bird dogs with him. He insisted all this was for protection as well as aid in tracking violators and making arrests. But some folks thought he should have had a sawed-off pump gun and German Shepherd rather than a double barrel L.C. Smith and pointers. Besides the sport, he always had partridges and whiskey. Some called it loot; he called it fringe benefits.

One day, Officer Mapp came upon this old shanty and under the rotten flooring found a coarse cloth sack. He might not have given it a second thought except for its strange letters and symbols. He opened the sack and found an odd assortment of objects including a dog skull, bones, fish scales, rocks and several dolls made of grass. The dolls were beautifully crafted, and he wanted to take one to his granddaughter. But something told him not to do that—perhaps the safety pins and nails stuck into the head.

No one would routinely connect this to Lizzie nor admit to recognizing the existence of heathen powers. However, everybody thought Officer Mapp made the right decision when he burned this building so no moonshiners could use it. Sometimes the best solution to things one cannot understand is to put them behind you and forget them.

I would not have thought of these things had I not been in my attic going through old letters and other treasures and smelling moth balls, when I came upon my cowboy hat. And woven in its withered straw was the perpetual memory of Lizzie Bibbins.

THE TRICKLE-DOWN EFFECT

Charlie and I stood there, he in his brown and white oxfords and me barefoot with my nickel in my pocket, and we licked our cones as equals.

If one desires to be deluged with memories, sweet and sour, the place to go is the local cemetery. This is especially true in small, rural areas where everyone knows or is related to everyone else. The tombstones are chapter headings in a table of contents describing the saga of a community, and if you look and listen, they will tell you more than names and dates.

Usually I amble around the cemetery after paying my last respects to a friend or relative, and I suppose I will do this more and more, if I am fortunate enough to live to an overripe age, until a time will come when I no longer have this privilege.

My most recent visit was occasioned by the death of a friend of fifty years—a friend when I was penniless and futureless—a friend who defended me in my more controversial days.

After the burial, I wandered away from the outskirts of

the cemetery into the old middle ground. Here the trees are larger, and the moss on the listing granite tombstones is richer. Somewhere in this heartland is the cemetery's first occupant, whom I always seek. It is here I began on this day and walked around in ever-widening circles— remembering and imagining.

Soon I came to the grave of Vivian Bailey, with his wife on one side and his lifelong, unmarried friend, Harvey Gilding, on the other. I had seen Mr. Bailey and Mr. Gilding sitting at a glass-top table with black wrought iron chairs eating lunch together at Miss Winnie's Sandwich and Ice Cream Shop in Belle Haven on innumerable occasions. Mr. Bailey was a car dealer who sold Chevrolets and Cadillacs. It was simple in those days. Each vehicle came in standard and deluxe versions—no other choices, except color and the number of doors. In good years, the farmers and watermen bought Cadillacs, in poor years, Chevrolets. One could not buy a big Chevrolet that cost more than a small Cadillac. There were no salesmen and no promotions—the customer took it or left it.

Most of the tombstones bore familiar names, and now the memories were breeding memories in a geometric fashion, but we will stem the tide a bit and I'll try to concentrate on one of the more interesting paths back through this granite local history.

Moving on, I passed the tomb of my Turner great-grandparents. A few markers farther on were the graves of twin brothers George and Harry Poulson, age 21. George had been lynched for the murder of a schoolteacher. But then with due consideration, the mob decided that it was probably Harry who was the culprit, so they hanged him also. Nearer the perimeter, where the shrinking fields began, was the Albertson plot. This family had a long and curious history in the community. My attention was on a large and beautiful marker bearing the name "Charles James Albertson."

I remember Charlie well, even though he had been ten years my senior. Now, a half-century later, I think of him as a happy youngster—frozen in time by death, never growing old.

It was also in Miss Winnie's that I had my first real impression of Charlie, although I had noticed him many times before. I was there not for lunch, but to thumb through baseball or hunting magazines, reading as many as possible before purchasing one. Mr. Bailey and Mr. Gilding were there when Charlie drove up with the white top down in his blue Chevrolet convertible, purchased for him by his father, James, from Bailey's Chevrolet. It was a beautiful, exciting car and it certainly outclassed the transportation of his peers. I also re-member the double-dip ice cream cone with walnut syrup, and a cherry on top, that Charlie or-dered. Anticipating the purchase of my weekly single, I was awed by this show of wealth. I suppose he noticed my envious look because he took a nickel from his pocket, threw it on the white marble counter and invited me to pick a flavor.

After ordering my usual, vanilla and chocolate mixed, Charlie and I stood there, he in his brown and white oxfords and me barefoot with my nickel in my pocket, and we licked our cones as equals.

It is interesting how wealth elicits various reactions from those that do not have it. Some express envy and disdain, while others are respectful and admiring, and I suppose a lot depends on the personality and ambitions of the observer.

Charlie lived in a big house in the better part of town and obviously was well off. His parents were very respected and pillars of the community; they were always on boards such as the hospital, the home for the poor and various charitable institutions. One got the feeling that because of this wealth the Albertsons were genetically a touch above ordinary working people. Perhaps they were.

Anyway, this wealth didn't adversely affect Charlie's attitude. He was always friendly to the less affluent children of the neighborhood, and one day he took Elmer Leroy Jr. and me for a short ride in his convertible. It was like riding in the back of the family truck, sitting on a couch.

Charlie loved sports, especially baseball. He was tall and left-handed, and this is one reason why he usually played first base. And I always thought he liked this position because he was in love and his girlfriend could sit on the sidelines and be close to him. Charlie was so good at baseball that some say the minor leagues were after him.

But after preparatory school at an academy up north, Charlie joined the Navy when the war began, and his baseball career was not to be. I cannot recall the last time I saw him, but every beginning needs an ending, and as I looked at his memorial on this sad day, I futilely searched my memory for this missing finality.

Charlie's father was arrogant, and I think this was because his money was "old money." It had been in the family for as long as anyone could remember, and the privilege, power and respect it collected, like barnacles on an uncoppered boat, had affected him.

There was a rumor among the "old-heads" about how this all got started. Those people are all gone now, so I can't verify the beginning of this tale, but will tell you what I have heard.

It seems that just before the Civil War my great-great-great uncle, John Custis, was a wealthy sea captain and merchant. He traded as far away as India in his four-masted schooner, and he sailed from his home on Folly Creek on the seaside of the Eastern Shore peninsula. In those days, about a century and a half ago, this small body of water was a port of entry, and there was deep water in the inlet between the barrier islands, Cedar and Metompkin.

Captain Custis was on his way home from India on a final voyage before retiring. (On the way out, he had sold his warehouse on the Thames and on the return journey disposed of his holdings in Barbados.) His cargo of tea and whiskey was worth a small fortune, and this did not include all the gold and silver he had collected or the precious gems

26

he carried on his person.

With him on this last voyage was his first mate, George Albertson, who had started sailing with the Captain as a child. Captain Custis had taken Albertson on as a cabin boy after he had been orphaned at the age of about ten. He was treated like a son and pushed through the ranks in a preferential manner, even though his abilities did not justify the pace of his promotion. Because Captain Custis did not have a son, he probably thought of Albertson as his own. There were letters from Captain Custis to his wife that would have implied this, but they were lost when the old home place burned, around the turn of this century.

Now they were returning from a two-year voyage, and all that remained was entry into Folly Creek from the vast ocean. After this, Captain Custis would retire and the schooner would belong to Albertson.

The channels and bars change quickly on the seaside of the Eastern Shore, and two years in the life of an inlet between the Barrier Islands is a long time. And in the captain's absence, a violent hurricane had reshaped the entire oceanside of the Eastern Shore peninsula. This could be the reason that Charlie had a convertible—and could afford a double-dip cone. The schooner hit a bar and was wrecked with a loss of all the crew except my Uncle Custis and the first mate—Charlie's great-grandfather.

As the ship was beaten to pieces in the surf, the two survivors floated ashore on debris. What followed was witnessed by two children of a sharecropper—Jessica Sturgis, a girl of ten, and her older brother who had been sent to Metompkin Island to gather wood chips.

When the two men were beached, there was some distance between them. The Captain, being older, barely survived. As he was slowly reviving, the younger mate began to walk the beach. When he came upon the old, half-drowned man, Albertson picked up an oar from the flotsam and killed him with repeated blows to the head. He went through Captain Custis' pockets and then dragged the body to the shore of the inlet allowing the ebb tide to return his mentor to the ocean.

Albertson subsequently claimed that his Captain had been lost and did not realize his heinous act had been witnessed by the two children, who were afraid to tell their story. It was only when Jessica was on her death bed eighty years later that she dared reveal what had happened.

The wreck was salvaged by Albertson and he became a wealthy man. Soon he married and the dynasty had begun—born of the sea and destined to die of the sea.

The Albertson family, in succeeding generations, became prominent in the social life of the community. When George Albertson died, his son Richard inherited the family's ill-gained wealth and the status it purchased. Richard Albertson was Charlie's grandfather. He also became a sailor of sorts and joined the Coast Guard. It seemed that the sea was still in the Albertson blood.

The Coast Guard is not exactly the French Foreign Legion, and many local people were able to serve their country in a military capacity without leaving home. I think the reasoning here was their familiarity with the marine environment, which was advantageous to the service.

For years, a series of Coast Guard lifesaving stations and lighthouses existed on Virginia's Barrier Islands, which run north and south, protecting the mainland with high dunes and wide beaches. The stations' purposes were many, and the Coast Guardsmen who manned these lighthouses and stations had various duties, such as patrolling the beaches, which were the eastward boundary of the United States, preventing shipwrecks and helping in rescue operations. Eventually, as the whim of politics demanded, enforcing drug and alcohol laws, mostly by trying to prevent illegal importations, also became their duty.

Richard Albertson was smart, or perhaps cunning would be a more accurate description. Even as a seaman he seemed to live better than his peers. He was always better dressed, or had better transportation—or had a newer bottle of whiskey or rolled a few more smokes than his otherwise equals.

Albertson did a commendable job patrolling the beaches on a mule and saving shipwrecked maidens and other unfortunates—as did many others. But he was promoted more quickly than his fellow coast guardsmen and rapidly rose in the ranks to became a Chief Petty Officer, which was the highest ranking local Coast Guardsman. His rise was so rapid that he was the youngest CPO in the history of the service, and it was suspected that the family's political connections were partially responsible for this.

Of course, as a CPO Richard wasn't getting rich from

his pay. However, his lifestyle seemed to change as prohibition arrived. When he came ashore, he was as dapper-looking as a well-dressed Mafia don. He had grown a little black mustache, spit-curled up on the ends, and he smelled of French cologne. He was always met at the dock by his wife, wrapped in furs and driving the family car, a large black Packard. He was obviously living in a manner not ordinarily afforded by a Coast Guardsman of any rating or rank.

My great-uncle Joshua was also a Coast Guardsman, and he and five other men worked under Chief Albertson, who decided where and when the patrols would be made at the mouth of the Chesapeake Bay, the purpose of which was to catch rumrunners. Initially they enjoyed some success at this. The Coast Guard patrolled at random, and, theoretically, the captains of the contraband boats would not be able to predict the schedule of prowling authorities.

However, Uncle Joshua said that the number of arrests gradually dwindled, and, eventually, they never even saw a rumrunner to chase, let alone catch. This failure disturbed my uncle. He was not that patriotic, he just liked a good chase, whether raccoons, rabbits, women or rumrunners. But there was no local shortage of alcohol.

Chief Albertson retired from the Coast Guard early and was obviously a wealthy man. He lived in splendor until he died around 1935 and left a 300-acre farm to his son James, Charlie's father, who became a farmer.

When the war began in 1941 farming was considered to be an important occupation—as Napoleon wisely noted, "An army travels on its stomach." However, James didn't raise much in the way of crops for the war effort, but he received an unusually large allotment of diesel fuel for his fishing boat and his farming operation. He had a barn full of 50-gallon drums of this rationed commodity, and it seemed that every time you looked down the road, more was coming.

About this time James began offshore fishing at night. He must have made a lot of money at that because he built a new house while most folks were economizing because of the War. He could get material, no doubt reserved for people of his high social standing, that was unavailable to most poor folks. My grandfather could not get tin for his barn to keep his horses dry or nails for their shoes, but steel beams were shipped down on a railroad car for James' new house.

My Uncle Lewis (by marriage) used to hang around Willis' Wharf, where James kept his boat. His leg had been shot off during World War I and he was old, so he couldn't do much to help the war effort. However, he wanted to play a part so he figured that he would use his spyglass to keep a lookout on the Bay for submarines. This was about all he could do except pick a few tomatoes. Potatoes were just too heavy for him.

Uncle Lewis never came to any conclusions about James Albertson. As a matter of fact, he never came to many conclusions about anything. He did tell me, however, about Albertson's going into the ocean to fish several nights a week. Many wondered why Albertson would load his boat with 50-gallon barrels of this precious fuel just to fish

31

boat with 50-gallon barrels of this precious fuel just to fish a few miles offshore. It seems he never caught many fish but used up a lot of diesel fuel. My uncle noted that James Albertson only took along one person at a time to help in this offshore night fishing—usually a drifter. On several occasions, the drifters never returned to the dock after a night of work on the ocean. Uncle Lewis always said he thought they were "drifting" in the ocean. Uncle Lewis said he would never go out into the ocean at night with all those German submarines patrolling the coast. According to his logic, "Those Nazis are apt to board you and steal your fuel, or worse."

I looked at Charlie's memorial that day, remembering his double-dip ice cream and the blue Chevrolet convertible, and I thought it was sad there was no tomb to go with the marker that commemorated his brief existence, and I thought it especially sad that Charlie was an only son—a progeny whose personality had seemed destined to add a missing sweet ingredient to his family's sour heritage.

I read it one more time:

"In Memory of our Son,
Charles James Albertson,
who gave his life
for his Country,
May 27, 1925 —
December 25, 1943."

It was a very costly monument.

32

FRIED BLACKBIRDS

*In death Aunt Rachel looked even more frail than in life, and her withered
frame was lost in her pine box,
posthumously purchased with her fat pig.*

As a boy growing up in a rural area in the 1940s, most
of my time was spent outdoors—weather permitting—and it
took pretty inclement conditions to keep me inside.

We roamed the fields and woods and prowled through
all the abandoned houses and barns, inventing games and
pretending we were hunters. This primeval hunting instinct
was encouraged by the country way of life, which depended
on it for sport and, to a certain degree, subsistence. Of
course, our first weapons were the timeless sling shots and
bows and arrows. Then several of us pooled our resources
and invested in a Red Ryder lever-action BB gun.
Sparrows, starlings and blackbirds were our main targets.
Robins and redbirds (cardinals) were strictly avoided. We
took turns shooting and didn't do much that would offend
the bird watchers.

The hunt and the stalk appealed to me, but I didn't like
to see birds killed without good reason. I felt then, as I do

now, that everything destroyed on this planet must be put to good use.

But Aunt Rachel was to change all this and give meaning to our way of life. She was the daughter of a slave, and I estimated her age at approximately 150 years, give or take a decade. She was a toothless, skinny, ragged lady who loved children no matter whether they were black or white, and this was not because she was almost blind and couldn't see them anyway. We often stopped by her shack, inconspicuously tucked away under the eaves of an old growth pine forest, for a cookie or bread crust with jelly. She would light up her pipe, sit on her porch steps and tell us of her own children, all of whom had died long ago of extreme old age. Eventually she learned that we had a BB gun and requested we bring her some birds to eat and said she would give us a penny each for sparrows and three cents for blackbirds. She especially liked the big boat-tailed grackles. This proposition interested me keenly because the consumption of the birds would justify their deaths, and my reading to date included a story about blackbird pie.

This was the beginning of our market hunting, and we bagged a few birds for Aunt Rachel. However, as so often happens, there arose a dispute among the founders of our meat-supply business. The problem was, I refused to shoot birds during the nesting season, and my partners would shoot the birds on the nest.

As a result, I sold out my interest to my cohorts—one of whom later became one of the most notorious murderers in the history of Virginia. But now that my hands were

34

washed of this unsavory carnage, I was out of work, and I dearly missed the chase. During that nesting season of our feathered friends, I mowed lawns, gathered pop bottles, did other chores and finally saved up enough money to buy a fourth-hand (or more) .410 gauge single-barrel shotgun held together with baling wire and Mason jar rubbers. When the blackbirds had finished their propagation and began to gather in flocks in the fall cornfields, I was ready for business. There were, however, serious economics to consider. The ammunition for the gun cost about six cents a shot, as opposed to a nickel for a pack of 100 or so BBs, and I had to get about three birds per shot to make a small profit.

I kept Aunt Rachel supplied with birds that winter, and one day she asked me to try them. When plucked of their black feathers they were as golden yellow as a purebred white Leghorn. Fried up very crisp in a spider of hog fat, the grackles were as good as anything I had ever eaten. They were so crisp that you could eat bones and all. How Aunt Rachel managed—she had lost her last tooth around the turn of the century—I don't know.

Then one bleak February day, when I had a few birds for her, I got on my bicycle, threw the merchandise into the basket and rode down the path to her house. That something was wrong began to dawn upon me; her hogs didn't squeal as usual when I made my appearance. In fact, they were gone. A window was up and the checkered chicken feed-bag curtains were whipping in the breeze. Aunt Rachel also was gone, along with her few possessions. Later I learned that she had died a few days before and was now "laid out" in the Baptist Church on the other side of the railroad tracks. I decided to visit her for the final time, even though I knew it would be a traumatic experience. I rode home, put on some clothes without holes and went into the church at the appropriate hour, when I knew others would be there. Besides the preacher, there were only three other people, and I never did learn their roles, but I suspected that there was a dollar or two in it for them.

In death Aunt Rachel looked even more frail than in life, and her withered frame was lost in her pine box, posthumously purchased with her fat pig. The thought came to me that some people live too little, and some people live too long. Moderation is preferred so you will not see all your children leave you alone in an indifferent world so ready to capitalize on your last act.

This hiatus in my market hunting did not last as long as my grief. The upturn in business started one day when I met old Alfonzo Watson on the road in front of my house. He lived on a farm outside of town and came in once a week with his mule and wagon to get groceries. He always had with him, sitting on an overturned bushel basket, a beautiful, young, golden-haired woman purported to be his wife. She was never known to speak to anyone, and no one ever spoke to her. It was not that she was unfriendly. It was just that she was shy and, I suspect, somewhat restricted by her mate. I did notice, on occasion, when she encountered children, you could see a slight sparkle in her eyes, and if you looked closely you could see the corners of her mouth turn up ever so minutely. No one knew her origin or anything about her except what they saw. This disparate couple didn't say if they were married or not, and no one dared ask. But there was a suspicious generation gap or two between them in addition to their being complete opposites in physical appearance—differences that exceeded gender and age.

Mr. Watson had been in World War I and not only limped from a bayonet wound but also had acquired a nervous twitch from being gassed. He was always dirty and bedraggled and, as far as I know, never had a good hair day. Prior to the war he had been an avid waterfowler but, as a result of his injuries, he could no longer pursue the sport. How he kept up with his young wife was always a mystery.

When Mr. Watson saw my shotgun on the handle-bars of my bicycle, he halted his mule and cart and offered me one dollar in advance for a pair of black mallard ducks. They, of course, were the best eating of all waterfowl. He had good taste in more than one way, despite his grizzled appearance and physical handicaps. He wanted these birds for his Thanksgiving dinner, and I set out to reconnoiter my hunting grounds and make plans the next day, the last of October. I now felt better about my career and realized that waterfowl was the real blue-chip stuff of market hunting.

No sooner had I spent the dollar than the first of many setbacks occurred; namely, a warm spell set in and all the ducks stayed well offshore in the Chesapeake Bay, sunning themselves, for about two weeks. It was just like summertime—I think you call it Indian Summer. However, I still had plenty of time. Plenty that is, until the baling wire on my shotgun broke while I was trying to ford a creek, and the fore end of my gun was lost in the mud and water. I tried for days to find it, finally dredging it up with a clam rake.

Thanksgiving was now only two days away, and many of the ducks had left—the first wave of the annual two-part migration. Thus, it was necessary to tell my client that he would not get his birds on time. He was understanding and said a Christmas duck dinner would be just as good. With a one-month reprieve to find and shoot two ducks, plans were made, and I started baiting with corn. I couldn't shoot them any sooner than mid-December because the old man had an ice box, and they would only keep so long. (Freezers were unknown in our area at this time.) Many birds were feeding, and it was decided that the time was about ripe for a shooting. That Saturday morning found me with my shotgun down at the dock, ready to go to the duck blind in my leaky old rowboat. However, on stepping down into the boat, my foot went right through the bottom, and the repairs set me back several days. My luck didn't change. Christmas came and went, and first one thing and then another kept me from filling my first order as a waterfowl market hunter.

I had shot a few off-brand ducks, and I offered the old man three shell ducks or four coots in place of the two black mallards, but he was a connoisseur and would not accept a substitute. It seemed I was never again going to get into range of a decent duck. However, in mid-March my luck changed.

One of my neighbors, Lester, had shot my pet hound just because the dog had used his yard for toilet purposes. The blast didn't kill him, but one of the pellets from the shotgun tore off a piece of his ear, and every time I saw it I tried to think of a way to gain revenge. Being a staunch believer in the Old Testament, especially selected parts like "an eye for an eye," getting even was religiously mandatory, but it was difficult to figure out the most fitting retribution.

Then one day in early April, when all the wild ducks had headed north for the season, an idea came to me. My neighbor had a flock of tame ducks he tended carefully, and they were pampered and fat. Often they would wander into the field in back of our homes, where I had shot my first rabbit the previous winter. The edge of the field was bordered by a ditch and scrub trees so that it was not readily visible. You can guess what was on my mind, but I couldn't just go out and do it, because each time I fired my gun my neighbor would come out to see what I was doing—if he was sober.

Some reading had been forced on me lately, and one story that stuck with me was *Peter and the Wolf*. I suppose the animals and the wild environment caught my attention, but the theme gave me an idea. Each day I would go out into the field and shoot two times at a tin can. Each time my neighbor would come out to investigate. After I did this about three times, he didn't come out anymore. About two days after the last conditioning session, his ducks were missing from the pen and I knew where to find them. With two shells and my shotgun I went into the bushes and across the ditch to where the whole flock of ducks was contentedly gleaning a cornfield. Two quick shots and two big fat Muscovy ducks were in the bag. My neighbor, who had been conditioned as expertly as Pavlov's dogs, never even came to his back door.

I took the ducks to a secluded spot in the woods and picked them. This was necessary in order to disguise the barnyard look. These domestic fowl were black and white, and I carefully removed all feathers of the latter variety and left a few of the former so the carcasses would resemble the elusive and delicious wild black mallards.

The overdue order was delivered to old man Watson with the explanation that the ducks were too fat to fly north with their wild brothers and had decided to spend the season here. And because I was so late on delivery, I thought it was only fair that I pick them.

He admitted as to how they were indeed fat, but seemed a little suspicious until he came across the black feathers purposely missed in the picking.

Later that week we met on the road. He stopped his mule, told me how good the ducks were and ordered another pair. The young, golden-haired girl just sat on her bushel basket and said nothing. I agreed to do my best, but this time I would not accept advance payment. It is surely the most tiresome of labor to work for something if you have already spent the earnings and have a deadline to meet. This is what they call "unearned income."

It was hoped that Lester would shoot my hound again, mandating the "an eye for an eye" religious thing, but my hound wouldn't go within a hundred yards of my neighbor's house, so I never filled this order.

In another and better world, perhaps we will all be vegetarians, but I had developed a lust for blood to go along with my capitalism. I sought out business even though it was illegal. Actually, I think the illegality of it made my new enterprise even more interesting. It was an exciting feeling to be both predator and prey. It was sort of like being plumb in the middle of the food chain.

The next season I thought I would seek professional guidance. Actually, this was contrary to instinct, because I always like to do my own figuring out from scratch. But civilization itself is a result of knowledge passed from one person to another, accumulating over the centuries. After all, I was using a shotgun that someone else had invented and someone else had manufactured, so it would not be cheating too much if I didn't invent everything myself and obtained some experienced advice on the slaughter of ducks.

There were several market hunters in the area, but the most renowned was "Captain" Jack Melson, who had fine-tuned waterfowl hunting for profit into an efficient business. Actually, his title was nonmilitary, just a local honorarium bestowed on certain people who lived past fifty or so and earned the respect of their peers.

Captain Jack, whose biggest boat was only about eighteen feet long, was not only an expert at hunting ducks but he also knew how to do it in such a manner that the finished product was more palatable to the consumer. And he knew how to mass-produce his product—just like Henry Ford—except on a slightly smaller scale.

He pointed out to me that if you shot ducks or geese while they were on the water, you were less likely to get lead shot into the breast. The angle of the trajectory was also important; if you were level with the birds, you would have more shot in the heads of the birds and less in the mud and water. This is simple logic, once you think about it, but when hunting to feed a family and not for sport, these refinements become important.

Corn was the best bait according to Captain Jack, but he also used sweet potato culls. This illegal bait was put out in a line so you would have a better strafing effect from your shot, which consisted of nails, nuts, bolts, as well as lead shot.

I wanted to look at his duck blinds, so one day he put me into his eighteen-foot boat and started up his one lunger. The two-foot diameter flywheel revved up to about one hundred rpms, and we went out into Craddock Creek to see his duckblind.

In the bilges was a mixture of mud, corn, blood and cylinder oil that sloshed around like a giant soup as we headed out. He docked the boat under the blind, and we climbed up and into the camouflaged box. Ducks were flying everywhere, and the thought occurred to me that someone might want to sneak in there someday and do a little poaching while the owner was in church or at a KKK rally. When I asked him how he prevented this, he gave me a sly smile, banged the tobacco out of his pipe, and stuck the stem into one of the many holes in the pine boards. "You see, Billy, every once in a while, nothing regular you understand, I just take my 30/30 Winchester and practices up on this blind. Most people know this, so it just ain't much fun for folks to shoot from my blind."

Captain Jack always knew what ducks were thinking. He was famous for that. I got the notion that he always knew what boys were thinking.

ON THE WAGON
WITH TOM SKINNY

However, at that time my goal was not to record or write anything but just to be in the country and away from the city.

The first I heard of prohibition came from one of my agricultural colleagues, Tom Skinny. Actually, quite a few of my first acquisitions of knowledge came from Tom. I didn't realize it at the time, but he was giving me verbal jewels, one-of-a-kind treasures, and I don't think I ever thanked him. Of course, he didn't look upon these unilateral discourses as anything of value. I doubt he could even read. Now, a half-century later, I am beginning to realize the merit of his tales and I would certainly put some flowers on his grave if I knew its location, provided he really was buried.

When I first got to know Tom, he was 80 or so. He was born a slave but soon freed. This is not to say that emancipation upgraded his economic or social status to any marked degree. He was in rags and destitute when I first met him and in the same condition a few years later when he

44

died. Of course, I didn't read about him in the obituaries—I just missed him one summer and was eventually told that he had "passed." When I learned about this from Aunt Lou (Aunt Lou knew everything), I couldn't work, so I hid out in an old walnut grove, where slaves were buried, and cried all day. I really missed him, not because of this sudden literary void in my life, but because he was my friend.

I admit that I also cried all day when my cat died, and she was as close to me as Tom. Children tend to value all friends equally, and the evils of comparisons and gradations are a product of growing up in the competition of the modern world. But the big difference as I saw it in those post-depression days was that my cat didn't have to worry about whether or not it would have a meal on any given day.

Most of my memories of Tom and his tales were created while we sat on a wagon and ate our lunches together. It was here that I listened, learned and unconsciously stored the information that enabled me to write these pages.

At that time my goal was not to record or write anything but just to be in the country and away from the city. During the war my parents worked in the shipyard in Newport News, Virginia. However, I did not like the city (I like cities even less now) and spent all my summers, at a minimum, living with my country relatives. In fact, at times urban life would get to me so badly during the academic term that I would cross the Bay and move in with one of my country relatives to complete the school term in a more appealing environment.

I did not like enforced education but actually learned more in the rural schools than in the city. There were four different grades in one room, and the dedicated teacher would go from one age group of students to another so that everyone gained a smattering of something.

There was a large coal stove in the middle of the room, and it was tended by one of the students. He was paid a few cents per day to come in early to fire it up and keep it stoked. I always coveted this job, but in retrospect doubt that I was dependable enough, because sometimes, after a few weeks, I would miss my family and decide to go back to the city for a while. The only job I was offered around the school was to help the cook set the table for lunch. My pay was to be allowed to lick the pots. What a pleasurable sensation it was to lower a big five-gallon pan over my head and lick the chocolate off the inside. These lunches were wonderful; but lunch beside a potato field with my friend Tom Skinny, away from school, pleased the soul as well as the palate.

I met Tom on my Grandfather Turner's farm, where I was sort of an apprentice trying very hard to become a decent field hand. Perhaps more accurately, we each became aware of the other's presence in a potato field. I was in the transportation department and Tom was in the excavation department. I drove the two mules hitched up to a four-wheel wagon that rode up and down the field collecting bags of potatoes. I qualified for this position because I was too young to handle the loading of the 100-

pound sacks or to dig alone. Besides, the mules were smarter than I and so well trained that my grandfather figured they could teach me something.

Tom was so old that he wasn't much at loading the sacks of potatoes onto the wagon. So, being an independent sort of person, he dug the potatoes, for which he was paid about three or four cents per bag, and his efforts were directly related to his pay. However, as a geriatric laborer, his prospects, economically speaking, were less than bright.

After getting out of school for summer vacation, the first farm crop to be harvested was Irish (white) potatoes. This started in mid-June and continued on until some time in July, depending on the weather. The potatoes were "dug" in two stages. First, a mule or horse (my Turner-side of the family always used mules and my Custis-side always used horses) pulled a single plow right down the middle of a potato row. This loosened the soil, and some potatoes were spilled out on top. The field hands followed and filled baskets with a combination of picking up the exposed tubers and digging out the remainder. It was a rough job, and one definitely needed a manicure after a day in the potato field.

This same procedure was followed for red sweet potatoes and the delicious Hayman (suitable for home use but not for shipping). The white potato was commercially the more important crop. Men, women and children participated in the harvest. Frequently, children helped their parents and all ages were represented. Some mothers even brought along infants and toted them around or stuck them into a basket lined with potato sacks while working in the fields. I recall one robust gal, July Belle, who stopped midmorning in the middle of her row to go home and have a baby. Later that afternoon she came back with the child and finished her row.

The black women were the mainstay of the actual potato digging. They wore uniforms that always consisted of a bandanna wrapped around the head "Aunt Jemima" fashion, a long-sleeved shirt, pants and a dress over everything. The pants were useful, because one was down on all fours most of the day. The dress was of no value for hiding any anatomy, but obviously was worn as an ornament to preserve the femininity of the digger.

There was usually an assortment of mongrel dogs and a goat or two tagging along behind their owners. Digging potatoes was truly a family affair.

My grandparents lived on their small farm, and I initially went home with my grandfather for lunch. Actually, it was more like a dinner in substance. It was the brevity of it, I suppose, necessitated by the persistent calling of duty in the fields, that gave it this minor characterization. Early on I noticed that most of the field hands, including Tom, were brown baggers. They would, at noon, take a little time off to sit in the shade of the woods bordering the fields and eat their lunches. Being an early romanticist, I decided this was the way to go. I convinced my grandmother to put some food in a bag for me so I could eat in the shade of 200-year-old walnut trees with the field hands. Usually it was a slice of cheese and home-cured ham

tucked between the halves of a huge yeast roll. This was accompanied by a pint Mason jar of fresh milk, and there was always a piece of cake or a slice of pie. She designed these lunches with items that needed no refrigeration, except for the milk, which I placed in the middle of a branch[1] in the walnut grove where the cool running water kept it fresh.

The mules also had lunch. I parked them, as instructed by my grandfather, in the shade of the trees bordering the potato field, and about two quarts of oats were put into each of their nose bags. A bucket of water was taken from the branch for them, but my grandmother always cautioned me not to drink it.

It was much cooler in the shade, and the big green-head horse flies were not as vicious in the diminished light. To be on the safe side, the mules' tails kept up a prophylactic swishing, and occasionally their skin would twitch or they would stomp the earth with a foot to temporarily dislodge a persistent fly.

It was in this setting that I sat on the back of the wagon and had lunch with Tom Skinny and listened to him talk about old and better times.

Tom, or perhaps I should say Mr. Skinny, was slightly built and the features of his face were more Caucasoid than Negroid. However, he was so black that he made his brethren look almost white, and I would guess that if you held a light meter next to his face and kept it away from his gray hair, it would be difficult to obtain a reading. The best

---

[1] A freshwater creek

way I can describe his color is that it was similar to the hue of a new tin wood heater. Perhaps it is not good form to mention a character's color in a story anymore; nevertheless, there are times when an imaginary blend of all hues into a homogeneous futuristic monotone person doesn't allow for a proper telling. This story, however, has a direct legitimate relationship to color, so I must ask your forbearance, whatever color God made you.

Tom always called me "Billy Boy" although I cannot recall the first time I ever saw him, nor can I recall the first story he told me. I really do not think he consciously meant to tell anything in particular. He just liked to talk and he liked me. It is equally true that I liked to listen, and I liked him. I certainly know that there is some possible benefit to being friendly with the boss' grandson, but I firmly believe our friendship was not based on economics. To me, we were the same age, same color and in the same profession.

Early on I had an inkling that whiskey was bad stuff for a person to drink, and there was some sin and wickedness invariably linked to its consumption. I am sure that this was imprinted on me by my grandparents' puritanical philosophy on such things. But evil subjects made good stories, and I vividly remember a couple of Tom's tales about this liquid and how it was against the law to own it, let alone allow it to touch your lips.

Tom recalled for me one day, while we were sitting on the wagon, a story about the good old days of prohibition, when he worked on the water at night and on the farm during the day. His nocturnal job was as a crew member on

Josh Evans' motor boat. Evans was a rumrunner and hauled whiskey to his landing from the big four-masted schooner that periodically anchored at the mouth of the Chesapeake Bay. I don't know why sailboats were used to bring the whiskey from the Caribbean and other sources to our shores, but this was the common practice.

Josh Evans' vessel was the usual Chesapeake Bay workboat: designed for oysters, crabs and fish. It was made of local pine and propelled by a converted automobile engine. Tom didn't really know about feet, but he said that Captain Josh's boat was about a mule and a wagon long, plus another mule tied to the back end on a short line. Thus, I now surmise that it was about 40 feet long. In those days, I just thought it was big compared to the little rowboat my father had built for me.

There were many local boats involved in the whiskey trafficking on the Chesapeake. Some came from the James and other rivers on the Bay's west side—others from the many creeks or inlets on the east side, which was, of course, the Eastern Shore.

Tom hired on with Josh Evans early in the whiskey business. He told me, weather permitting, they made about one trip a week. There were two other black crew members along with Tom. Actually, most rumrunners preferred black crews, not simply because they worked for less but because they were more trustworthy and less apt to talk about this illegal business.

Tom was wanting to get married, but first he had to save up enough money for a mule and a cookstove. The money in rum running was evidently good. Tom said, "I made as much in one half a night in dis as I would have in scratching out eight or ten doubler rows of taters in de hot sun all day." He also said he received a bonus pint of the merchandise for "medicinal" purposes after each run.

If the weather was moderate, Tom's job was an easy one. It was a two-hour run down the Bay with no work. After arriving at the schooner, about one hour was needed to load the whiskey. The run back was a little longer because of the load. Then there was the unloading in Captain Josh's maintenance warehouse at Salt Works on Nassawadox Creek, and everyone made an easy night's work.

If the weather was foul, not uncommon in the winter months on the Chesapeake, the trip could be longer and more disagreeable. When I once asked Tom if he liked boats, he replied, "Well, Mr. Billy Boy, I loves boats. I just don't like de water."

Then he told me about one especially rough night when they were heavily loaded and a squall came suddenly out of the northwest, the worst of the quadrants on the Chesapeake. Tom and two other crew members were sent below to man the bilge pumps. Water was coming through a missing hatch cover and the seas had loosened some of the caulking in the planks and there was a crisis of some magnitude. (I don't think it was as bad as Tom told it.) The water was kept at bay, but Tom and his crew members were getting tired—manning the pumps is hard work. Finally, they came on deck to tell Captain Josh they were too exhausted to pump anymore. Captain Josh did not argue, he just went below while Tom held the wheel. After a few minutes he reappeared on deck donned in a double breasted suit. Naturally, Tom asked why he dressed up. The reply got things moving again. "Well, men, I always promised myself that I would die in a coat and tie, and that's what is going to happen to all of us if you don't get back to pumping."

However, the weather was not the factor that gave Tom the biggest scare of his whiskey-smuggling career. It seems the "revenooers," who were government enforcment agents, and the Coast Guard were desperate to catch some of the violators. The decision was made to infiltrate the ranks and pose as legitimate (or illegitimate, depending on your perspective) bootleg dealers. In the mentality of the times, it was decided to paint black some white law enforcement people to pose as the crew. I imagine the government didn't hire blacks to help catch the violators, because they didn't feel they were qualified for jobs such as spies. Of course, now you can legally drink all the whiskey you want and it is illegal to discriminate in employment, whether it is spying or teaching school.

Anyway, word got around that there were some enforcement agents painted up black and posing as crew members on the local boats, and the schooner captains began to take precautions.

One night, after they tied up to the schooner, Captain Josh went aboard to take the money (in this business they didn't take any credit cards). Then, he called after Tom and another crew member to come aboard. Tom said he always "ran a little scared in dat business." Usually he stayed in Captain Josh's boat to stow the cargo. He said, "Dat big boat wid dose sails is just like a slave boat and I did'n want nuttin' to do wid it." But duty called, so he climbed up the side and made himself as inconspicuous as possible. No sooner had he put his feet on the deck than a lantern approached; it hung in front of his face for a while and was moved from side to side, closely inspecting him. On the other side of the glare and holding the lantern was a large hand with two fingers missing. Then Tom's eyes made out a huge Chinaman. Tom said, "He was a brick taller dan ya

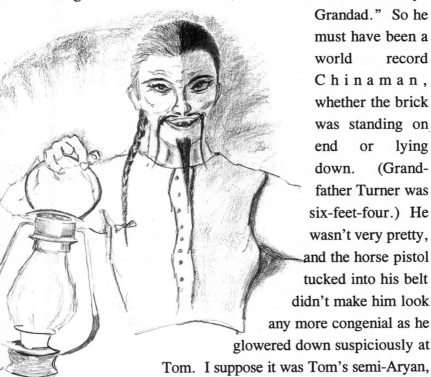

Grandad." So he must have been a world record C h i n a m a n, whether the brick was standing on end or lying down. (Grandfather Turner was six-feet-four.) He wasn't very pretty, and the horse pistol tucked into his belt didn't make him look any more congenial as he glowered down suspiciously at Tom. I suppose it was Tom's semi-Aryan, non-standard, Negroid features that caused suspicion. Anyway, after a few moments of terror and thought (the terror was Tom's), the Chinaman licked his thumb and rubbed it down Tom's cheek in a scrubbing motion while he intently watched the reaction in Tom's eyes. Then the Chinaman held the lantern up to his thumb to see if any black paint were on it. A ragged-toothed smile came upon the wide mongoloid's face and he jerked his head toward the barrels of whiskey, a sign that Tom had passed the test and could begin loading.

Tom said to me as he chewed on a chicken foot, "Yas suh, Billy Boy, dat de only time dat I ever tanked de Lord for bein' black." At that time, I didn't know what he meant, but gradually I learned, conformed, and later reconsidered.

After getting back to Captain Josh's warehouse, the "catch" was unloaded and stored alongside the oysters and potatoes. All of this was completed before daylight. The next morning there would be a sudden spurt of business on the wharf when strange vehicles would start coming to pick up barrels of "oysters and crabs."

This building was built on poles extending out over the water with a portion over the bank. It was like all other waterfront depots of the era, made of single pine planks, both on the floor and sides. The barrels also were wood. For someone with vision, this was a tempting opportunity, and as we were sitting on the wagon swatting flies and eating rat cheese and ginger snaps, Tom proudly told me another story connected with his rumrunning days. It turns out that he didn't really know the end of the tale, but he was proud to tell me of the time his cousin outwitted Captain Josh, who wasn't very popular with blacks or whites. If he had known the sad conclusion of the tale, I am sure that I wouldn't have heard about any of it.

Tom had a cousin named Joe Pie who went to the "city" to work at an early age. He apparently did relatively well and years later came back home on the train. His prosperity was obvious, not only because he had shoes and a matching belt, but also because he had two conspicuous gold teeth in the front of his mouth. He was, therefore, considered to be highly intelligent by his peers.

This prodigal cousin, like all returnees to the Eastern Shore who have been on great ventures to seek their fortunes in the city either temporarily or permanently, wanted to impress his friends and relatives. After hearing Tom talk about the whiskey business going on down at Josh Evans' wharf at Salt Works, he decided to steal some of the contraband. This would be a real feat and certainly take him out of the ordinary class of chicken and watermelon thief.

Actually, the way Joe Pie went about this does show some style. He did not merely break the padlock or pull off some of the pine siding, enter and haul off some barrels of whiskey. This would have been a one-time affair that he dare not repeat. Realizing that this would attract attention and flood the local market, he decided to conservatively embezzle in a manner that would give him a continuing supply of beverage and allow him to impress friends and relatives with his generosity over the entire span of his visit home.

Tom proudly related: "Joe went to the sto and git a 'ooger' (auger—or a hand-operated wood drill) an' a bit. Then he get a stick an a old pump pipe an a big jug. In the middle of de night when de tide be out he go under de house, right under de whiskey barrel. He don know where to go 'cause I always put de barrel in de corner over a knot hole."

The bit was used to drill a hole through the bottom of the whiskey barrel, which was sitting over the knot hole. When the prohibited liquor suddenly came through, a piece of pump pipe was pushed up to the bottom of the keg to use as a funnel. Although it was probably tempting to drain the whole barrel, he didn't. He only took about "two water pails" into the jug. Then he quickly inserted a plug, which was all ready, into the bottom of the barrel. "Joe done give everbody whiskey all summer. Den one day he musta go back to de city cus nobody seed him no mo," said Tom proudly.

Tom loved to tell about this. He told me that tale several times, and I think he wanted it to sink in about how his black cousin Joe outwitted Captain Evans. I was always glad to hear it, and Joe Pie was one of my first real heroes—sort of like Robin Hood, I suppose.

About a quarter of a century after Tom died and a quarter of a century before I wrote this, it came to pass that Captain Josh's old warehouse on the wharf had to be torn down to make way for a marina and a lot of plastic yachts.

It had been unused since his death about fifteen years earlier. His children all went away to college and did not return to their home to live. So his paraphernalia (fishing gear, barrels, baskets and old boat motors, etc.) sat there and gathered dust and pigeon droppings for years.

Eventually the land was sold and the old building that had seen so many gill nets, barrels, potatoes, crabs, oysters and wild ducks, not to mention whiskey, was emptied and dismantled. In a pile of discarded contents were several oak barrels that a farmer friend of mine wanted to use for salting fish and scalding hogs. He loaded the barrels into his truck and took them to his farm near Buzzards' Glory, my birthplace. Noting that something was still in one barrel, he opened the top and peered in. What he saw made him decide not to use any of the barrels for fish or hogs. Peering out of the brown liquid as he peered in was a human head staring straight up with an open mouth, and the first thing the farmer saw was two gold teeth sparkling in the first sunshine they had seen for a half century.

I'm glad Tom Skinny had "passed" long before this whiskey barrel was opened up. He probably never would have told me about Joe Pie and his auger if he had known the conclusion of the story. There is nothing wrong with a little pride, and facts should never take it away.

FROGGY'S GARDEN

A flock of laughing gulls was working a school of bait fish that the ebb tide had channeled between two sandbars a few yards off shore.

On the Eastern Shore in the '40s and '50s, when school was out for the summer, not many of us traveled abroad or went to camp. We went to work. This was not only a necessity but a luxury after theoretically spending nine months in school. (Six was actually my cumulative record.) However, there were many ways youngsters could earn money in a rural setting, either by land or by sea, when their lives were not distracted by academics.

The agricultural environment afforded opportunities for labor on farms, and this mode was more accessible to most children. If one was not independent-minded, nor ambitious, there were hourly remunerated positions available pulling weeds, spreading manure or loading produce onto farm trucks. Of course, if your parents owned the farm, your pay may have varied from nothing to minimal. More interesting to me was harvesting produce, such as tomatoes, potatoes or strawberries, and being paid by the unit, resulting in a direct correlation between effort and reward. This also allowed one to be his own boss to a large degree, always an attractive feature.

While farm labor had its appeal, I preferred to wrest a living directly from nature, especially when it pertained to salt water. A primitive instinct compelled me to harvest the waters for anything that was marketable.

That's what Elmer Leroy Pruitt Jr. (we always called him Elmer Leroy for short) and I were doing in the summer of 1944. We had some crab pots set out and we were catching a few crabs to sell. Then we decided to rig up a trotline. We thought there would be more action in this, and it would give us something to do while we waited for the crabs to crawl into our pots.

A trotline is a long rope with an anchor at each end and a series of hooks on short lines secured at intervals in between and baited with pieces of fish. Crabs are attracted to the bait, and one pushes the boat along the line from one hook to the other, gently lifting them off the bottom. As the crab is busy eating the bait, one carefully raises it to the surface, puts a net under the crab and dumps it into a basket. We had received a lot of advice on how to do this from our old friend Froggy Upshur, who knew all kinds of ways to catch things on the water.

We hadn't had our trotline out many days when it happened. We were still in the experimental stage and spent a lot of time untangling lines and hooks. But we were having fun with it and catching a few crabs. One morning, about halfway down the 300-yard-long line, we felt

something a little bit heavier than usual, and we pulled it up slowly, hoping to see a big fish or a turtle. As we peered expectantly into the depths, we saw something strange. Here was a big, furry creature on our line, or at least it was big relative to a crab, and we didn't know what to make of it. We didn't know whether we had found some new species of animal or what. It really scared us. We pulled it into our skiff along with several crabs, which were eating on its eyeballs and various other delicate parts that tasted so good the crabs forgot to let go.

As you know, the delicious blue crab makes its living from eating rotten food of any kind it can find on the bottom. It is not very particular. How the meat gets to taste so good I don't know. That seems a contradiction. I've often seen poultry picking maggots out of rats and such things, and fried chicken always tasted good, so I guess in nature's recycling you get a purification of sorts.

Anyway, we pulled this thing in, and it was a horrible sight. The hook through its mouth was framed with a big, toothy grin. There was fur all over it, and it had a semi-human alien-looking face. Being partially eaten up did not enhance its appearance. We didn't know what to make of it at first and were relieved to some extent when we saw that it had a tail. We finally figured out that it was a monkey, even though we had no idea what kind. And the origin of this foreigner was a puzzle. How was one to know if it had swum all the way over to the Chesapeake Bay from Africa, had escaped from a circus, or what?

After collecting ourselves, we decided to take this

critter ashore and bury it, knowing if we told anybody about it or if anyone saw us with it, they would begin to wonder. It was our intent to wash our hands of this whole affair as soon as possible and try to obliterate it from our young, impressionable minds. A Christian burial was performed, even though it was a monkey and it may have been that Muslim rites would have been more appropriate. Anyway, we got rid of it and did not go back out to our trotline that day. Our concern was that something else strange would be hooked, and we didn't want to face it.

So, after the burial, we called it a day and sat down on a pine stump on the bay shore to think about the experience and calm our nerves. Elmer Leroy took a half-smoked Camel and a kitchen match about the size of a tenpenny nail out of his shirt pocket. He struck the match on my bare heel, which, as usual, amused him. Routinely, I put my shoes away after school was over, which meant I could get by with one resoling per year. It also meant that by July my feet were thickly calloused. I was upwind of his smoke, shucking a few oysters we had picked up, and we were silent and thinking.

It had been a wonderful day before the monkey was hauled aboard. A flock of laughing gulls was working a school of bait fish that the ebb tide had channeled between two sandbars a few yards off shore. Now their raucous cries seemed to be directed at Elmer Leroy and me, and, with their help, it gradually dawned on us that somebody had toyed with our emotions. Naturally, we didn't want to go around accusing people, because that would allow the person who did the tricking to have even more fun at our expense. The further astern this matter the better. We did, however, have some ideas about how this thing had transpired.

Froggy's cousin, Rufus Upshur, was an assistant zookeeper up in Philadelphia (I think he cleaned cages), and occasionally when an animal died and he would be down for a weekend, he'd bring it along and show it to Froggy and us boys. He knew none of us had ever been to a zoo, and the opportunity to see these things was a treat, even though we would rather have seen them alive. One time he brought down an anteater, on another occasion a parrot. We figured that possibly he had brought this unfortunate monkey to Froggy, who decided, because he couldn't eat it, to use it to his best advantage, which was, of course, playing a joke on somebody. This time it seems Elmer Leroy and I were his victims. That's what we thought, but we were never sure. We never discussed this with Froggy or anybody else. It was like being kidnapped by aliens and taken for a ride on a UFO—we kept it to ourselves.

Elmer Leroy and I lived in town, on the main street that leads to the cemetery and not far from Froggy. Our town, Belle Haven, was typical of most Eastern Shore towns, with a row of houses on large lots bordering each side of the street and woods or farmland in the back. A lot of folks had gardens, and because it was during the war years you could have called them Victory Gardens. I think Froggy would have had a garden regardless of whether a war was on or not, because he came from a farming family. He was like my father and many other folks who had a rural background and for one reason or another had to move into town but still liked to hold on to the growing experience. His garden was different though; it had not one weed in it and, except for a few ladybugs, not one insect. The soil was like granulated sugar, colored brown. He kept it perfectly smooth, well-watered from his garden hose and well-manured from his cow. He always had butter beans, pole beans, tomatoes, watermelons and usually a few exotic vegetables, such as parsnips or Chinese cabbage. This garden was his pride and joy.

The boys around town liked Froggy. He was always joking and playing with us and was always ready to help when we needed experienced advice, whether it was smoking a possum out of a hollow tree or catching a crab in the Bay. He loved the outdoor life and having innocent fun—he was a boy himself.

Elmer Leroy and I decided one day it was time we returned some of Froggy's jokes, because we assumed he put the monkey on our trotline, even though we were not certain about this. We spent a long time trying to figure out what to do that would have some real class to it. We finally narrowed it down to three options: we'd kidnap his cow, take it out in the graveyard and tie it to a tombstone; we would get all the goldfish out of his pond and take them to his neighbor's pond; or we would do something to his garden. After serious consideration, we decided on the last, because we knew this was his most sensitive spot. Of course, we didn't want to damage it to any degree—that would be vandalism. We just wanted to be subtle and worry him with absolute minimal destruction. The remaining question: how to do this?

One Saturday night, at the movie at the Idle Hour Theater, we saw something on the newsreel about Big Foot out in Oregon. The film showed some of the damage it had done and the supposed tracks of this monster, which nobody had ever shot, caught or even seen. So, we decided we would work along those lines and see if we could develop our own Big Foot. First we went down to the Wilkins Bros. Garage and got an old truck tire. We rolled that home and cut off two big slabs and carved on them with a butcher knife and made two huge feet complete with toes and pads. I would guess they were about a size 18. We even put in a few little scars and some arthritically deformed joints in some of the toes, just to make everything look authentic. We then fastened these homemade paws to the bottom of a pair of worn-out gumboots.

In order to do this thing right, we didn't immediately zero in on Froggy's garden. First we went down to Silver Beach and walked along the sand where people could readily see these tracks. This was about five miles away. Then Big Foot gradually moved in closer to town and Froggy's garden. One night he walked across a plowed field down by the cemetery. A couple of nights later, some distinctive prints were left in a pile of wet clay that was the by-product of a new two-seater on the Tilghman farm. After several more preliminary excursions on the outskirts of town, people began to discuss this situation at the country store and the barber shop. Froggy heard about it and asked us if we knew anything about these footprints people were seeing. Any knowledge of them was denied, of course, but we did take a keen interest in it from then on, and we knew the plot was getting thick and the time ripe.

The tracks began to get closer and closer to Belle Haven and, after about a week of encroachment, it was decided the time had arrived to go right through Froggy's garden. One night, when we knew our old friend was out 'coon hunting with Albert Beach down Occohannock Neck, Big Foot walked through his garden and knocked down one of his butter bean poles. No real damage was done, just enough to show that something big and potent had been there. The following day, Froggy saw us just as we happened to be riding our bicycles past his home. We didn't get a chance to say anything as he excitedly described the footprints in his garden. He took us out to the scene of the crime to show us and said he sure hoped the thing would not eat his pig.

While being carefully guided by Froggy through the garden, we realized the prints weren't deep enough. A lot of pressure was needed on those footprints to give the impression that their owner was enormous. Elmer Leroy, a little on the fat side, wore the paws this first time, and I climbed on his back. That brought us up to a good weight, but not enough to really sink the tracks sufficiently, so we experimented and finally used a potato sack carrying about eight bricks to increase our weight. Now, between Elmer Leroy toting the bricks and my climbing on his back, it left a nice deep print. It seemed to me that this beast with the size-18 foot would probably weigh something like 300 or 400 pounds.

Froggy seemed to be nervous but didn't say any more about it that day. I think he hoped this critter was just passing through and wouldn't be back. That was not to be, however, because two or three nights later it was decided to get a little bit more of a rise out of him, so Big Foot went through his garden again. This time we mashed a few of his tomatoes, dug a hole or two between the rows and stepped on one of his big cabbage plants. The next day, we visited Froggy again on a pretense of business of some kind. He was really upset this time. You could see his concern growing about this creature's taking up permanent residence in his neighborhood. So he asked us if we would come to his home that night, sit in the barn loft and watch for this thing to come back. We were delighted that Froggy was getting really worked up and thought this was a wonderful joke. Sitting in his barn all night knowing that nothing was going to come didn't appeal to us, but we always did what Froggy asked us to do, because he was a good friend and could not be abandoned in his time of need. Besides, observing his torment close at hand would make it all worthwhile.

After the sun had gone down, all three of us went out to his barn and sat in the loft on some bushel baskets peering through a crack overlooking the garden in the back of the barn. It was a hot, humid night, and the bugs were coming in everywhere between the weather boarding.

Initially we enjoyed being there while this joke was taking effect on our friend. Of course, nothing showed up. After a couple of hours the watch was terminated. Froggy went back into his home, and we went to ours to bathe and put Raleigh's ointment on our gnat and mosquito bites.

The next morning, Elmer Leroy and I agreed this joke needed some fine-tuning to make it appear more realistic. We got the idea to gather animal dung and form it up to look like some kind of superhuman excrement. Plenty of raw material was available for this, since Froggy had a big coonhound and a cow. A ten-quart bucket of it was gathered and a busted bicycle tube was located. The omnivorous mixture was stuffed into the tube and pushed on through with a hoe handle acting as a plunger. Proper twists and twirls were added, as if it had gone through a set of extra huge intestines. A nice little pucker was formed on each end, with peristaltic constrictions in between. This sculpture was carefully situated in the middle of the garden. A potato rake was used to make some scratch marks and cover it slightly as cats do.

Next, we took a big bear trap with teeth in it and let it snap shut into the side of one of Froggy's prize watermelons. The trap took a tremendous bite out of the melon. It looked like some huge jaws had done this. Earlier that day Elmer found a dead dog on the highway, run over by the Greyhound bus. We pulled it apart with the potato rake in such a manner that it looked like it had suffered a lot while being eaten alive. It was left in a scuffed up area in the lettuce bed, and one would think that a life and death struggle had taken place right there. A couple more butter bean poles were knocked down, and Big Foot left a lot of tracks. That would be enough for one night.

The next day we needed to see Froggy about borrowing his plow so we could work up a garden for old man Sturgis down the street, and the first thing he wanted to do was to show us what happened to his garden the night before. This was, of course, what we expected. He was really getting nervous about this, it seemed, but the problem was he wanted us to come back and wait again that night. Neither of us could turn down our friend. After all, he had just loaned us his plow. At dusk we came back and brought some sandwiches, soda pop and candy to help relieve the monotony. Again, all of us sat on bushel baskets peeping out the back of the barn.

It was not long before Froggy's wife, Flora, came out the back door, hollered out that he had a phone call and said for him to come on in. He went in where it was nice and cool with his Montgomery Ward air conditioner stuck in the window. Elmer Leroy and I were left out in the barn watching for the Big Foot that wasn't going to come by, so we just sat and scratched as the mosquitoes and gnats feasted on us. It was a long phone call and a long night for us. Finally Froggy came back out. He sat with us for a short while, and then he decided to call it off for the night. This was welcomed by us, because it was beginning to get on our nerves sitting there waiting for a hypothetical creature and getting all whelped up from the insects. Now a true dilemma faced us, and we didn't know what to do. If we immediately stopped the surveillance, Froggy, knowing that we were getting bored and bitten sitting in the barn, would put it all together and realize that Big Foot was not real. After much thought about this, it was decided to let the joke gradually die a natural death and the footprints would get farther and farther away and finally cease.

Big Foot made footprints the next night on the other side of town, and somebody up there saw them. Froggy heard about this and began to feel relieved that the critter was moving on. We did come back and pay him a farewell visit with no damage and, a few nights later, moved up the road about two miles and left some prints on a freshly seeded lawn. Our old friend began to get the idea that Big Foot was headed north. Finally, after a couple more nights of watching, Froggy relieved us of our duty. This was welcome, because sitting in Froggy's barn and being eaten by bugs had lost its appeal. We now decided that the time had come to let Big Foot become extinct. The size-18 paws were buried in back of our clubhouse and have never been used or even discussed since. As far as I know, they are still buried there.

As Froggy aged, he became somewhat feeble, and in our sympathy we gradually imagined that we had done something unrespectful by playing a trick on our old friend who had done so much for us. Our rationalization was, of course, that he played tricks on others whenever he had the chance. Still, it just didn't seem right for boys to trick a grown man who had been their friend. We had worried about that over the years but never had the courage to confess.

And then came the time when Froggy had a stroke. It affected his speech a bit, as well as his mind and his movement. No sooner had he recovered as much as he could than he had another stroke and it became apparent that life was closing the doors on Froggy. By this time, Elm, as he had decided to call himself, and I were in college (Elm later dropped out and worked on the water), and when we were home we always went to see our sick friend. Finally we could stand it no more. During one visit, we confessed to Froggy that we were the ones who had tampered with his garden and that he was actually looking at Big Foot. But we never mentioned the monkey. He looked at us and laughed, as well as you can when you've been stroked out on one side. He said he deserved a joke to be played on him and that it did create some interest in his life and we shouldn't worry about it.

About six months later our friend Froggy died. I came home from college and they let Elm out of jail for the day so we could pay our last respects to our friend. After the funeral we went by his house to sit with his friends and relatives. As usual there was a lot of food—pies and cakes and rolls—with everybody sitting around eating and reminiscing. When it came time to leave, his widow reached Elm and me an envelope and explained there was a message inside from our departed friend and teacher. We knew there wouldn't be any money, because he didn't have any, but were really touched that he had left us a note. The envelope was taken to our car and eagerly read by the light of one of Elm's kitchen matches. Here's what it said:

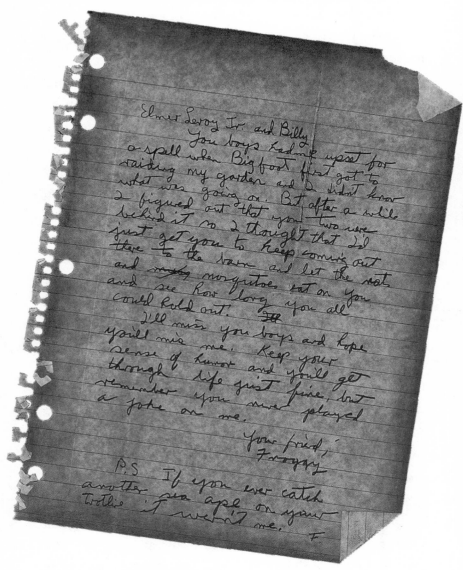

He was invincible, and we were glad of it.

THE LONG ARM

*Smells have a way of doing this—little index cards that lead you back in time
to vividly re-experience sounds and views filed away somewhere
and somehow in a maze of neurons and synapses.*

As a youth, whenever I wanted to awaken early in the morning, my alarm clock was set the previous evening. Certainly many others do this, but the difference was in the clock. Mine contained no springs, sprockets, gears or pendulums and was built into my body—it was my bladder. Of course, everyone has this same organ, but I learned to program mine to tell me to get up whenever I desired. To do this, all that was required was a simple calculation that considered two factors: the time of retirement and the amount of water I would drink before going to bed.

This memorable morning, which is the beginning of my tale, the four glasses of water consumed at 10:00 p.m. called me to duty around 5:00 a.m. And this was a morning I did not want to miss; it was the first day of legal duck hunting for the 1948 season. I do not mean to imply that my partner Lorenzo Jones and I had not prematurely shot a few birds; we always started early. With this infraction no

75

longer a consideration, we were now one step closer to being legal and could concentrate more on hunting and less on watching for the law.

Ren, as he allowed me to call him, and I had been companions in the chase for two seasons. He was about twenty years older than my thirteen, but seemed to enjoy my younger company. There are those who have suggested that my strong back and weak mind were useful to his wicked ways and this was why he took me under his wing. Whatever the reason for this generation-gapped alliance, I had fun and learned a great deal, even if a large part of this education, as is the rule in life, was negative.

My clothes were pulled on enthusiastically: three shirts and two pairs of pants. To keep the cold November air of the Chesapeake Bay out of the holes in the knees, the top pair was reversed. This worked fine except when nature called. Lastly, I checked the inner-tube patches on my boots and, not seeing any toes, grabbed my gun and went down the street to Ren's home. As I opened the back door and entered the kitchen, I could see that he had already shaved and was meticulously parting his hair, and Vitalis was heavy in the air. He was a man who put a big store in ritual and insisted that he could not shoot straight when his hair was out of order.

His toilet complete, our guns, decoys and bait were loaded into the back of his worn out farm truck, and we headed out of town to the dock on Kilmontown Cove. This was a small body of water that simultaneously opened onto Occohannock Creek and the Chesapeake.

We always put out bait for ducks, which was illegal then as it is now, but it did make things interesting. The preferred bait, which seemed to agree with the old squaws and other diving ducks we hunted, was weed seed. In those days, when farmers harvested soy beans, the weed seeds were collected separately from the beans and not allowed to go back into the soil to sprout the following spring. Now, progress has made it cheaper to forget the weeds and saturate the land with toxic chemicals that do not affect the crop; they just cause the consumer to die a few decades early while the runoff into the Bay and creeks kills the eel grass, clams and oysters.

The real advantage to using weed seed instead of corn for bait was that it was less visible from the air. This was an important factor to consider because the law was just beginning to take unfair advantage of innocent violators, such as Ren and me, by using seaplanes for enforcement of unjust laws. From the vantage of the air, a grain of yellow corn was as conspicuous as a brightly polished gold nugget.

When we arrived at the dock, fresh bags of bait were tied to the pilings to soak a few days, so it would not float, and the already saturated bags were put into the boat. It seemed only fair to feed the unfortunate birds we were harvesting.

Day was breaking behind the pines lining the bay shore as we headed out to our blind a mile or so away and a quarter of that distance offshore. We passed the No. 9 buoy and then the fish trap, which was about midway. This trap was not functioning at this time of year. Roger West had removed all the netting after he made his last haul of croakers and trout in October. Now there were only the six-inch diameter poles about ten feet apart, stretching perpendicular to the shore for 300 yards.

These poles offered us some degree of security from the game wardens in seaplanes. At the end of the previous season, they had saved us when a plane landed in our homeward bound wake after an illegally fruitful day. We simply went between the row of poles to the safe haven on the opposite side as the plane tried to approach. Unable to go between the poles, the plane was forced to take the long way around in attempting to board us. We would then just push our skiff between the poles to the other side. We were very close, but unreachable, and for about a half hour we had a trying conversation with the wardens. The pilot, a mean-looking, smallish man, seemed irritated, but his companion, who appeared to be well over six feet, just smiled and said, "I'll see you later," as they flew off into the sunset in frustration. We paid no attention to this routine, standard salutation.

Soon we were in front of our duck blind. This was essentially two rows of pine poles about five feet apart, arranged in an open-ended rectangular design about eight feet by twenty feet. Onto each side of these poles were nailed narrow boards with cedar boughs and myrtle bushes pushed between them for camouflage. At the closed end, a wooden box large enough for three people was fastened to the poles, about ten feet above the water. From this vantage point we would shoot and look.

We put out the decoys in the exact configuration Ren dictated. Careful attention was given to the proper pairing up of hen and drake, not that the ducks I have seen were that particular—certainly not like the monogamous Canada goose. They also were counted carefully to be certain that the number of stools was odd. This was very important according to Ren, who always insisted that no duck worthy of being shot would decoy to an even-numbered rig.

With these arrangements complete, we retired to the comfort of the snug blind to enjoy breakfast, the sport and the vista.

The broad view of the Chesapeake with the sunrise on one's back was an experience that alone justified the preparation, long and short term. The mingled smells of salt water, cedar and bayberry were also there—subconsciously and permanently anchoring this scene into one's mind. Smells have a way of doing this—little index cards that lead you back in time to vividly re-experience sounds and views filed away somewhere and somehow in a maze of neurons and synapses. This view of the Chesapeake is still there and will always be. Only the perception of the experience will change.

It was still calm that morning, but Ren said the weather would change for the worse—which would be better. This is the way of duck hunting. The Bay is known for its vicious fickleness, but that day things other than the weather would change.

Many ducks came to our decoys—mergansers, buffleheads, scoter and, the beautiful to see and hear, old squaw. Some of the less fortunate did not leave, and we exceeded our bag limit. But we would not hunt the following day, so why not shoot that future allotment while we were there?

Around 4:00 that afternoon we loaded our gear into the boat to head home. We were getting low on fuel, because we used more than usual chasing cripples and retrieving ducks. But we had enough to get to the dock.

From the eastern perspective of the "shoreman," the Bay is even more beautiful at dusk than dawn, and the colors in the west were beginning to coalesce along the horizon as we headed in. It had been a great day, and we were enjoying the voyage home.

We had not gone far when a suspicious speck appeared in the northern sky. It was a seaplane. However, we had been through this before, so we headed back for the safety of the fish trap poles, now 200 yards on our stern.

The plane saw us and immediately set its wings like a lone Canada goose that had come upon a flock of its brethren. We just held onto a fish trap pole as the plane taxied up on the other side. We recognized them and they recognized us from our previous confrontation. Ren came right out and told them the facts, "You two wasted a lot of taxpayers' gas last year doing end runs around the poles while we just went between—you might as well run along home now—we'll do the same 'cause you're not going to come aboard our boat."

They readily agreed and in a friendly way said they would get us in the open some day and check us out. They were good sports and good losers.

The plane left and said goodbye with a dip of its wings and was soon just a speck in the southern sky and getting smaller. We started up our outboard motor and made a bee line for the dock. Then our luck changed as quickly as the seas on the Bay when a squall comes out of the northwest; our motor sputtered, then stopped. As feared, we had run out of gas. This meant we would have to pole our boat the rest of the way—not serious because in those days I could have poled to Baltimore against an ebb tide if I had possessed a pole of sufficient length. So I just took off a layer of clothes and set in poling while Ren lit up his pipe.

Things seemed to be going along fine—I was enjoying the poling and Ren was enjoying his smoke, but the hard part was yet to come.

After a few big pushes, I let the skiff coast along and looked back at our blind one last time before it was obscured by South Point. It was a pretty view except for one thing—the speck in the sky had not faded out of our existence but actually seemed to be growing larger. I mentioned this to Ren, and suddenly there were twice as many of us poling twice as hard because the airplane was returning. We headed for shore and the safety of the woods as fast as we could. Soon, however, all hope ebbed, and as the graceful seaplane glided to a halt between us and freedom, we realized we would be caught.

"Well," said the long, lanky warden, with a smile, as his towering frame stepped out onto one of the pontoons, "I saw you boys were having trouble, and we came back to help—I sure hope you appreciate it." I silently remembered his parting remark about eight months before, "I'll see you later."

You just can't hide a potato sack full of ducks in an open 16-foot boat, but Ren was trying. He tried to push it under the bow, under the seat, under himself, and I think he was considering how to stuff it into the empty gas can when the warden stepped into our boat and held up an identification card. He was putting it back into his pocket when Ren decided that the best defense was a good offense, which I am not sure is always true. There have been many times when I have seen a hound put his tail between his legs and save himself a lot of trouble.

"Now just hold on there!" said Ren. "If that's your identification let me see it—you can't be too careful now days with lots of imposters and criminals running around as thick as gulls." Ren seemed to have some knowledge of his rights, but I thought that at this particular time he should keep his legal expertise to himself.

Ren took the card and agreed that the photo was a good likeness, and I breathed a sigh of relief, thinking that was over. But it was not, I realized, as Ren drawled, "This says you are 6' 6", but how do I know that?"

The top 10 inches of the warden suddenly turned as red as our Montgomery Ward Sea King outboard motor. "Well, I don't have a tape measure, so you can just guess." Ren was not going to stop there, however. "My shotgun has a 32-inch barrel on it," said Ren, as he put it beside the warden's size-14 foot, held his grimy finger on the warden's leg, marked off another measure, and finally satisfied himself that he was not dealing with an imposter.

I just wanted to distance myself as far as I could from Ren, which wasn't far in a small boat, but I moved to the bow and sat on the locust sampson post.

Now it was the warden's turn, and he asked for the sack. He poured out the ducks and counted them. It was plain that there were too many, and Ren's promise to not hunt tomorrow and let the excess spill over into the future was ignored. My tender age and my tail between legs saved me as I answered all questions with a "sir." Ren got a summons, the big warden got the ducks, the little pilot got a laugh, and I got a warning.

After the warden said "see you later" for the third time, we poled on to the dock, lucky to have our guns. Ren's kids would not be eating ducks that Saturday night.

Ren didn't seem worried about the forthcoming court date. He went about his semi-useless life as usual, but I suspected he was mulling things over and something was incubating. The first thing I noticed was a crudely painted sign on the door of his worn out Chevrolet truck. It read: "Odd jobs done cheap—Lorenzo Jones" and I knew right away that was fraudulent advertising—Ren would not work for anyone under any circumstances except to help someone out free. He considered it demeaning to hire out his body for money.

A few days later, my cohort said he wanted me to come to court with him as a character witness. I explained that if I had to do that under oath I might get hit by lightning, drowned in the Bay or fall out of a tree. He said that he didn't think it would come to that, but if it did, just to tell about the good and forget the bad. That reassured me because the testimony would, therefore, be legitimately brief.

The day for the hearing arrived, and I was instructed to be at Ren's house early for the trip to the county seat of Accomac. I had assumed it would be the People vs. Jones and me. However, Hilda, Ren's wife, and their three kids—twins, plus a single—piled into the truck with us.

Hilda looked about as bad as I had ever seen her—she appeared to have been digging potatoes all day. Her clothes were threadbare, and her stockings had so many runs in them one might think she had worn them several seasons picking blackberries. She carried a black patent-leather pocketbook, which was peeling, and a paper bag of diapers and milk for their babies. Their faces were dirty with egg and pablum, and their noses could have done with a wiping.

It was a pitiful sight. I worried that the law might confiscate these children and send them to live with foster parents.

We arrived at the courthouse parking lot about an hour before the time of reckoning and Ren parked his old truck right next to the place marked "Reserved for Judge." We piled out of the truck. It was a relief to stand up because I had been designated to hold my foot over a rusted-out hole in the floor of the cab to keep the cold air out as we whizzed along the macadamized road at 25 knots or more.

Immediately I headed for the warmth of the courthouse. Besides, I didn't want anyone to see me with the Jones family. I looked back for Ren and he was letting the air out of his front tire—the one next to the judge's space. This concerned me because I knew I would be volunteered to pump it up. Ren always had an explanation for everything, and he logically told me that it was a worn-out recap, which was true, and it needed a rest. I sure hoped Ren would have an explanation for the judge.

We all sat on the front row in the courtroom waiting for the trial to begin. I had never been in one before and this new experience prompted me to sit and think about my life and where it was going, provided I didn't get locked up and go nowhere for awhile.

85

The feeling of having to be in a certain place at a certain time to have yourself judged and punished by a stranger is as discomforting as being stuck on a mud flat in the middle of the night at the beginning of ebb tide. And even though I was only thirteen and statistically had many years to go, I was reminded of another day of reckoning, in which my whole life would be evaluated by a bigger judge, and I became somewhat morose.

My thoughts were interrupted when we were all told to rise and an impressive looking man with gray hair and a long black robe like an Episcopalian priest walked in and sat on his "throne," which seemed at the time to be about ten feet above the level shared by Ren, Hilda, the kids, me and some other equally unsavory-looking people behind us.

Our case, or rather Ren's, was first on the docket, and the tall warden was present on the other side of the courtroom, which was where I would have felt less embarrassed. However, my allegiance was to Ren, and I was determined to stick by him.

The warden stated his case, which was rather simple: Ren had shot too many ducks. He did not refer to the bait or evading arrest as he told his side of the story to the judge and glanced sympathetically at Hilda and the kids, one of whom had begun to cry out as if in pain. Ren then took his turn and the judge tried to ask him some questions above the din. I could barely hear Ren explaining that all we did was to shoot the next day's limit in advance. About the time he got to the feeding-his-family part, Hilda's pocketbook tumbled to the floor and three pennies and a nickel fell out.

She sat the two screaming babies into the arms of the older one and got down on her hands and knees to pick up the money. The nickel had rolled over in front of the pulpit, and for an instant the judge started to rise to help her, then thought better of it. But one could see that he was being affected as he said to Ren, "Mr. Jones, what kind of odd jobs do you do?" "Your honor," replied Ren, "I do most anything that comes along 'cause I got to feed these children." I think that he was getting close to perjury at this point, but he did do whatever was needed to feed his kids, including not wasting grocery money on fines.

About this time Hilda pulled out of the paper sack a piece of chicken feed bag with flowers on it to wipe the nose of one of the twins. Immediately the baby started to sneeze amid its wailing. Ren was very apologetic as he explained to the judge, "Your honor, I'm sorry about the young'uns, but they are all coming down with colds."

The judge kept looking at the warden, who now reminded me of myself sitting on the bow of the boat, then at Hilda and the kids. I was beginning to feel sorry for the poor old fellow, obviously torn between a sworn duty to the people and his own personal humanitarian feelings.

After a few minutes of pounding out an unheard rhythm on the bench with four fingers, he seemed to gather his thoughts, and I could tell that the sentence was forthcoming. "Mr. Jones, I'm compelled to declare that you are guilty, but I'm not going to fine you, because if you had any money, which I don't think you do, you would need it for a new tire. And if I put you in jail, I think you would enjoy the rest. So I'm going to send you home with your family."

He took a hammer and hit something; then he left the courtroom and I guessed he went to his chambers to try to forget it all. Ren, Hilda, the kids and I went back to the truck. It was cold, but I pumped up the tire without complaint, eager to get out of town as soon as possible. Inside the cab, Ren was looking at some little red pinch marks on the twins' legs, and all of them were sneezing. I decided to ride home in the back of the truck because I didn't want to catch anything.

The following March, while preparing my shad net for the spring run, I started sneezing. The last time I had used the net, there had been phosphorescence in the water from sea nettles and jellyfish. This had dried to powder, and I had inhaled some of it. For a moment I thought I was coming down with something, then I remembered the trial and how the Jones' kids all seemed to have caught a cold instantaneously in the courtroom but were somehow fine the next day.

Ren, in a negative manner, was one of the most inventive and resourceful of my colleagues. If he had just gotten through the primer, he might have amounted to something and could have gone into politics or maybe even religion.

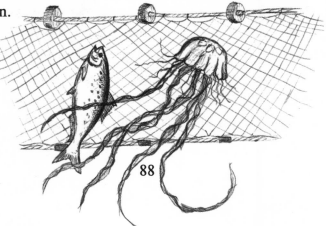

I TOLD YOU SO

His posture was reminiscent of a boomerang stood on end,
and he always carried his shotgun held behind his back with both hands.

The way from my home in the little hamlet of Belle Haven to my cousin's in the country was a hard-surface road for a few miles. When you came to the town of Craddockville and made a turn to go down the Craddock Neck Road, it abruptly became two miles of just plain dirt. Down this neck[2] lived my maternal grandparents and Aunt Dorothy and Uncle Melvin.

I would traverse this route on our bicycle to spend the weekend, or a week, or sometimes a whole summer with my rural relatives when the hustle and bustle of the three hundred or so occupants of Belle Haven encouraged me to go to the country for some relief.

When I say our bicycle, I am referring to the joint ownership of this vehicle by my sister and me. It was a girl's bicycle. It was secondhand and served us both as a

---

[2] A small peninsula formed by two tidal inlets and the Chesapeake Bay.

matter of economy. I was always concerned about my image while transporting myself on a machine designed for females, but other than that I don't think it had any effect on me. Besides, I usually had a rabbit or squirrel in the basket and a shotgun suspended on the handle bar. I suppose this and my hip boots dispelled any frivolous notions that any observers may have had. Evidently, my parents figured that it was easier for me to accommodate myself to a female bike than the reciprocal. We were definitely not a two-bike family.

Before the advent of the bicycle into my life, I made this trip by a combination of rides with the mail/ice delivery man to the town of Craddockville, which was a last outpost of civilization. I would then walk the rest of the way, unless I was fortunate enough to catch a ride in a horse and wagon or, rarely, a motor vehicle. Actually, I didn't mind the walk because of the wildlife along the tree-lined way.

I did not see anything except squirrels, rabbits, crows and an occasional covey of Bobwhite quail, but the soft dirt of the road was an accurate record of everything that had recently crossed. There were the zigzag paths of snakes; rabbit, squirrel and raccoon tracks; and occasionally the cloverleaf imprint of the fox. I took my time on this road and, with a walking stick in my hand, tried to unravel the mystery of every sign.

It was usually a hot, dry walk, and even though I sometimes had a nickel in my pocket for a soda at one of the country stores in Craddockville, I always saved it so my cousin Melvin and I could party together at a later time.

Thus, I was usually dusty, tired and thirsty when I arrived at my cousin's or grandparents' home.

There were several little intercepting roads along the main route. After you got past the outskirts of Craddockville, there were only two residences close to the road. One was an old shack with a perpetual column of smoke coming from a rusty stove pipe. I knew that it was inhabited by Bill White, a tall, aged, stooped and rawboned black man. I had seen him on several occasions when I had driven by his place in the relative luxury of the family truck.

I believe the first time I saw him was during rabbit-hunting season. It was only then that he would venture away from his house with his pair of aged beagles. He would stand in the road and wait for his hounds to chase the rabbit across the road. This was certainly the most advantageous place to be and a lot easier than plowing through the woods and briars.

His posture was reminiscent of a boomerang stood on end, and he always carried his shotgun held behind his back with both hands. Sometimes he would have a cottontail rabbit dangling limply

91

from his belt. After all, if you had been so fortunate and cunning as to bag a rabbit, why put it in a coat pocket where the world could not see it?

His snow-white hair was covered with an old Stetson. For efficiency, you may take it for granted that everything I describe about Mr. White was old. His many-layered wardrobe all matched in the sense that knees and elbows had long ago been worn away, and the remaining material surrounding the four holes was threadbare and faded.

He always carried either a stick and a pipe or a shotgun and a pipe, nothing more and nothing less. I remember distinctly that the shotgun was not an automatic nor any terrorist-type weapon but rather a hammer-type single-barrel. The fore end was held to the rusty barrel with several Mason jar rubbers, and the splintered stock was held together with wire.

Bill White never spoke when we motored by in the truck or lumbered by in a horse and cart. It seemed that his huge hands were permanently grown together behind him, precluding any gesticulating. However, my cousin and I thought that he should at least nod his head. Thus, one day when we were riding in my grandfather's horse and cart with our feet dangling off the back, we decided to get the attention of this obstinate old man. We knew that he would be in the immediate vicinity because we never saw him at the store, the post office or anywhere else, and we never saw a vehicle in front of his house. Retrospectively, I think his supplies were airdropped in the middle of the night.

We decided to call him Bill "Brown" to precipitate a

response to our recognition of his presence. We were justly proud of this clever play on words, and we devilishly executed this plan when we spied him standing by his porch in the shade of a tree in his usual posture and attire. We simultaneously called out "Hello, Bill Brown!" in greeting. We elicited no response from Bill White but did get the attention of our grandfather. The old horse was brought to a halt. Hame lines, I can assure you from the ensuing exposure, make an indelible impression on young white asses.

The following summer, while traveling this same route on a hot, sunny August day, I still had this experience on my mind as I tiptoed past Bill White's home, keeping as far to the left-hand side of the road as possible. I thought I had made it safely past the danger zone when a voice from the trees boomed out, "Hey dere, li'l white boy, come over here." I froze in my tracks for a while, but the command was repeated in such an authoritative manner that I was compelled to obey.

"Now don't fall in de ditch," I was cautioned as I walked on a pine plank across the mud and water, reminding me of some pirate stories I had recently read.

"Where is you going, boy?" was the first interrogative directed at me as I was about midway across the plank, which felt like a high wire. "I'm going to see my Grandpa and Grandma Custis," I innocently replied, and I was extremely eager to see them or anyone else at this time except this ancient descendant of African cannibals.

"Well, you better not fall in de ditch, cause dose Custis

folks has all got tempers."

Then he chuckled and added, "Well, I gis you dun larned dat," obviously recollecting the Bill Brown affair.

"Come over here and sit on dis old stump and tell me some tings."

I sat down as commanded and answered what was the equivalent of name, rank and serial number, imagining the feelings of a prisoner of war. Then, as he got into less official interrogation such as age, brothers or sisters, etc., I began to realize that things were not as bad as I had imagined and sensed that all this old hermit wanted was a little company.

My host (not my captor) realized I was thirsty and offered me some water. I eagerly accepted, and he straightened up with some effort to his boomerang ambulatory position and went to his hand pump. After a few coughs that gradually transformed into satisfying squeaks as the pump was primed, he filled a milk can with the cool liquid and handed it to me. Thirst quenched, I recognized the Pet Milk label still clinging to the vessel. This was the same brand of milk that my own family used, and I began to get an idea that maybe there was not an ice age gap between his existence and mine.

These Pet Milk labels always intrigued me, because each had a picture of the bust of a cow and a picture of another can of milk. On this smaller can of milk was also a bust of a cow and another can of milk, and so on.

Now, my cousin and I had gotten into many fights over

94

this label. He, being precise minded, insisted that there was a mathematical limit of seven cow heads and cans to this thing. I, being the philosophical type, insisted that they went on and on forever. I later learned that the words for this were ad infinitum.

Emboldened by the fact that in all likelihood I was not going to come to any harm that day, I queried, "Mr. White (and I was very, very careful to not say Mr. Brown), how many cow heads are on this can?"

"Well child," he replied, "I can't hardly see de can and I can't count neither so you mus ask somebody else."

He then added, "Dis here can is jus fer you and I goin' to hang it on dis here limb for nobody but you. When you is thirsty you jus stops here and gets youself some water. No black folks is goin to drink from dat can."

Assured now that I was physically and disease safe, I thanked my new friend and was now enjoying my importance. However, he soon continued, "You bes' run along cause dose Custis folks got hot tempers and you probably got weeds to pull."

He was right on both accounts, but as usual, I was expected to arrive unheralded sometime during the week, and I probably wouldn't have been missed for several days anyway.

Thus, I journeyed on, a little wiser, a little less scared, less thirsty and a lot richer.

From then on, whenever I traveled down Craddock Neck Road, I made a pit stop at Bill White's. My can was always hanging on the wild cherry branch, and the rusty, shallow well water was always as sweet as the Nehi strawberry pop in Ralph Custis' grocery store, where macadam met dirt in downtown Craddockville.

It was while sitting on his pine stump one day that this elderly field hand told me about the pet gray fox that he once had. But first I will tell you about this particular breed. Foxes in Eastern Virginia are either gray or red. Most people think of the latter when the subject comes up. It is much more abundant and the one preferred by the hunter. This is because they run before the hounds in a more or less straight manner. The gray, however, just travels in small circles and does not make the long runs that excite the true foxhound enthusiast. In one respect, the gray resembles the house cat because it can climb trees, and its claws are very sharp and somewhat retractable. Bill White insisted that they were just like cats and they also had nine lives. When he mentioned this to me, I readily agreed that cats did have that many lives; everyone knew that, but I was skeptical about this when it came to foxes.

Slightly surprised at my ignorance, he went on to tell the story of White Ear. It began about ten or twenty years ago (as I have said, he wasn't much at counting) when his chickens began to disappear. His flock (he wasn't sure how many he had) furnished him with all the eggs he needed, and when the hens quit laying, they ended up in the pot. It was a normal and expected, if not desired, thing to lose a chicken to predators once in a while. However, once he lost several in the course of a couple of weeks, so he began to sit by his opened window, shotgun ready, hoping to get a shot

at whatever it was that was gradually reducing him to
poverty.

Finally, one dark night while guarding his birds, he
heard a lot of squawking in the henhouse. In a few seconds
the commotion ceased and he strained to see a target.
Suddenly he saw one of his white hens being dragged across
the ground. He could not see what was doing this, but from
the direction of the movement he could estimate the position
of the killer. He fired and the hen's movement stopped.
With his lantern he went into the chicken pen and found a
gray fox, dead but still clutching its prize. He plucked the
bird and put it into the pot that night. He too had to cut his
losses. Because its pelt was not prime, the fox had no value
so he left the corpse there for the time being.

The next morning, after a fowl breakfast, Bill White
went to the chicken pen to throw the fox carcass out into the
woods. When he picked it up, he noticed that its mammary
glands (he didn't use that exact term) were full and he sadly
realized that he had executed a nursing mother, which like
so many other creatures, greater and smaller, was fulfilling
an instinct and perhaps a duty to nourish her dependent
young as nature dictated.

"I sho did worry about dat Momma fox's kittens," Bill White said, with genuine concern lingering in his eyes, years after an incident at which many people would not have blinked.

Then, after a pause in which his pipe received some careful attention, he continued. It seems that he knew from some earlier experience that the young would eventually begin to cry out in hunger. But this would take some time, so he waited until the afternoon and began to walk through the woods in places that seemed to him to be the most appealing to a gray fox. Finally, just before sunset, he heard a low and mournful cry. He proceeded in the direction of this sound for a distance, being careful to not overshoot the source, and waited. Then the cries became more frequent and, after a few more encroachments, he knew the sound was emanating from an uprooted hollow tree; it was here that he found two gray fox kittens, one of which had a white ear. I interrupted to ask why he called them kittens and he explained patiently:

"De reason you call dem kittens, Billy Boy, is dey is jist like cats. Now de other foxes (red) is like dogs and I call dem babies pups." And I recall other wise "ole-heads" who agreed with this distinction. From my own observation I have seen a gray fox climb a tree, and it did so as well as a cat.

Bill White gathered up these creatures, the orphaned offspring of his enemy, and took them back to his home. I would guess that he too was being guided by some primordial instinct, honed sharp by trial and error in nature's laboratory, which knows no respite and whose patience is endless.

He placed the fox kittens on the floor of his kitchen, which was also his bedroom, as well as the maternity ward for his house cat, who had a brood of kittens behind his cook   stove, which was also his heating system. And in a world of wasteful, unimaginative specialization, this is an example from the past of the beauty and efficiency of multiple functions.

As soon as he deposited the orphans on the floor, the cat came out with hackles raised and suspiciously inspected the new occupants. Perhaps she would have eaten them, but being amply fed on the abundant mice in the old shack, she went back to her offspring. Now the next step in this little drama does not amaze me, but what intervened in the mother cat's brain in the meantime does. In a short period, she again approached the fox kittens, this time in a more docile mood, and picked up one of the foxes by the scruff of the neck and moved it to her bed behind the stove. Being able to count to two at least, which put her on a par with the landlord, she returned and repeated the maneuver. This gave her a brood of six kittens, and they all began to nurse.

In the days that followed, the foxes became vigorous and aggressive, and it was apparent that they were detrimental to the nourishment of their step-siblings. Noticing this, Bill White decided to give away one of the orphans. Of course, he kept the one with the white left ear, which was a male.

This was only a temporary expedient however, and eventually all the kittens died of starvation. Now this part of the story did not bring any tears to my eyes, because I have real problems recognizing the need for domestic felines in a wildlife environment. But it is, of course, their keen hunting instinct that makes them so destructive, and fighting nature's instinct is a waste of time.

In those days, kittens would often end up in a potato sack with a brick for a companion to take them to the briny deep. There was just no money in the propagation of cats. And even though no one wanted more cats, the sex urge in all creatures was as hard to control in those days as it is now and no doubt will be in the foreseeable future.

With time, White Ear, as he was appropriately named, grew into a handsome adult fox. The shack was his home and his hunting ground, and mice were seldom seen. The old mother cat died, and he had his little microcosmic world to himself. Bill White shared his cooked food with the fox and they pleasantly dined together on most occasions. However, whenever raw meat was presented to White Ear, he would immediately take it behind the stove where he had a "nest" made from worn out potato sacks. If approached at this time, he would growl and instantly revert to a wild temperament. Otherwise, he was fond of human attention and would rub against the human leg, as cats have done since they first cast their lot with man.

Bill White and White Ear had a symbiotic, if not

pleasant, relationship for, as near as I could make out, three or four years. Then, within the space of a week, a disease, probably distemper, took the life of both of the old man's rabbit hounds and White Ear.

This was a great loss to my friend—except for his chickens, this was his entire family. He eventually replaced the hounds, but to find a gray fox, especially one with a white ear, would, of course, be impossible.

I cannot recall a visit when he did not mention White Ear, and he always insisted that gray foxes had nine lives just like cats. As I have said, I knew this was true of cats, everyone did, but I was doubtful about this privilege extending to canines, and my skepticism always elicited a "you'll see" attitude from the confident old man.

I had walked that dirt road many times and later graduated to a bicycle. Eventually, however, I acquired a secondhand Chevrolet that always seemed to be gasping steam as it passed the White residence. A gallon jug was kept there for this purpose, and my milk can was replaced with a pretty good-looking jelly jar clearly designed to fulfill two destinies. And, of course, I would have stopped anyway, even if I had no need. After listening to professors lecture at college, Bill White was as refreshing as his water.

One day, as I motored down Craddock Neck Road on five cylinders and recapped tires, I detected, in the straight road a mile or so away, the old man's angular image. It seemed as if he were anticipating my arrival, which was based on some probability due to my college schedule. I stopped my car, and he eagerly greeted me and then led the

way across the ditch to his old house, which was not getting any younger. He said he had something for me to see. We went through the shack to the chicken house out back, and without a word he dramatically allowed my eyes to come upon a gray fox skin nailed to the weathered door. Initially I saw nothing unusual about this, because he frequently had a possum, raccoon or rabbit skin nailed up on a door or the side of his house. As I turned to face the old man and saw his dentally sparse grin, I realized that he had made a point, but I wasn't quite sure what it was. I looked at the fox skin again and, as I stood there, my puzzlement became embarrassment and then amazement as I realized that one of the ears of the sun-dried hide was as white as Bill White's hair.

Enjoying the old man's gloating, I thought about my recent college course in statistics, his insistence that gray foxes had nine lives and my skepticism. And if these odds seem astronomical, consider two more facts: the fox was found dead on his back door steps without any sign of injury, and it was the left ear that was white.

THE OLD YELLOW HOUSE

It was here that I would arrive, neither expected nor unexpected,
with no invitation, no definite stay in mind other than days or weeks,
and no fanfare—just welcome.

The fantasies of youth embellished by time may twist and bend reality, but the final perception is the important thing, and nothing else matters. The facts are the bones, and the feelings one gets from any setting create the less definite but more malleable flesh. When the immature mind is absorbing, weighing and enjoying a constant barrage of impressions, there is no delineation between fact and fantasy—it is only when older that reason and reality begin to dissect the memories. And, many of my most pleasant and fantastical childhood experiences were in and around the "old yellow house."

Continuing down the dirt road past Bill White's home, one soon came to a fork. Straight ahead was Melson's Marsh, the land of ducks, geese, oysters and the Yahoo, a mysterious creature never seen but often heard on the saltwater marsh. The alternative to the left meandered through a beautiful mixed hardwood and pine forest until

104

there was, in another half-mile or so, another fork. Here, the road to the left went to my Custis grandparents' home, the other to that of my Aunt Dorothy and Uncle Melvin. This was my more frequent destination, because here were two cousins just a little older than I. But at that time, of course, this difference seemed like a generation gap. However, as I write this, more than a half-century later, we are all approximately the same age; the abrasive sands of time are a great equalizer.

Just as the woods ended, there was a dilapidated tenant shack on the right. In my lifetime it was used to store baskets and as a place to cut white potatoes into eyed slices for spring planting. This was done by old black women who would sit beside a tin heater on upturned baskets, smoking pipes, chattering and working. Prior to this, the shack was the home of a supposedly happy couple who worked in planting and harvesting for Uncle Melvin. They had no children, an unusual handicap in those days. One day, however, some altercation arose between them that could be resolved in no other way, so Jenny repeatedly stuck an ice pick into Solomon's back. He ran from their abode, fell into the middle of the dirt road and expired. The sheriff came and took Jenny away, and she was never seen again. A mule and a wagon were sent by someone, and Solomon was hauled away. Needless to say, he also was never seen again.

When this itinerant laborer died in the road, he lost a lot of blood, which soaked into the dust as his sweat had done in the fields. Afterwards, whenever it rained, the blood would reappear and remain visible until all moisture had disappeared from the earth. The old field hands told us this and we believed it, and thus we saw it.

On my frequent visits, therefore, it was with some trepidation that I crossed this threshold from the woods into Uncle Melvin's carefully cultivated fields. However, despite my misgivings, I always dug into this holy spot with my big toe and my walking stick. If there was moisture, the crimson stain always would be plainly visible.

From this spot, one could see in the distance the shimmering horizontal sliver of blue that was Craddock Creek, one of the many sinuous and sensuous inlets that penetrate the Eastern Shore peninsula on its westward side. Perched just above it and separated by sand bars and pine trees was a similar vision of the Chesapeake Bay, with the sky firmly holding everything sandwiched in place.

Between the woods and the water was a fifty-acre farm. In the middle of this parcel was my aunt and uncle's home, with its pale and peeling yellow paint, its four huge cottonwood trees and the usual complement of outbuildings, including a henhouse, stables, barn, outhouse and corn stack[3]. Depending on the season, this scene stretched before one as a green forest of corn, an umber plain of raw earth with thousands of laughing gulls following the horse-drawn plows, or a vast park peopled with field hands digging, toting or picking, with dogs barking and children playing and hollering.

---

[3] An outbuilding designed for drying and storing corn on the cob, also called a crib.

After leaving the legendary blood-soaked road, it was only about four hundred yards to this oasis in the midst of the tilled fields. At times I could smell fried chicken or hear my cousins' voices as I approached. However, it was absolutely impossible to arrive without recognition—even though I tried it many times, thinking that it would be the dramatic thing to do. The ever-present hounds (coon, fox and rabbit) would always detect me as a relative stranger (or perhaps a strange relative) and, in a friendly way, announce my arrival.

It was here that I would arrive, neither expected nor unexpected, with no invitation, no definite stay in mind other than days or weeks, and no fanfare—just welcome. To me it was only routine to change homes for a spell. Weary of the hustle and bustle of a town of three hundred souls, I would go to the country to work a little, to fight with my cousin a little, to play a little and to go without punishment when I am sure it was due.

I remember this home, my relatives' home, my home, as clearly as I do the one in which I now live. I know the precise location of the mouse hole in the pantry, the squeaky board in the kitchen, the cottonwoods, the barn, stables, chicken house, outhouse, the drain pipe from the shallow-well hand-pump on the porch, which, despite its squeaky protests, issued forth shallow well water for man and beast, and countless other details.

The entry into this home was invariably through the back porch, which led into the kitchen. There were no columns, no hitching post, no servants, and no sweet-scented magnolias. There was a semi-rotten plank of about ten feet in length used as a boardwalk when it was muddy. Grass did not grow in this well-trod ground next to the entrance, which was the hangout area for the chickens, cats and hounds waiting for kitchen scraps and/or attention. The bottom half of the porch was made of vertically placed pine boards, and the top half was screened. Inside the porch were a bench, a woodbox and the water supply—a delicious mixture of rust and water that must have kept everyone's hemoglobin at a peak. Under the eaves, there was a wooden plate running around three sides, and this was used as a

storage shelf for many things that my uncle had placed there for easy access. It held an interesting assortment of salves, elixirs and pills (for the livestock), bolts, nuts, nails, pocket knives, traps, shotgun shells, twine, baling wire, tire patches, beat-up and taped softballs, saddle soap, cultivator hoes, horseshoes and countless other necessities of farm life.

But it was the sense of smell that was first and most forcefully impressed on you. Wonderfully exciting aromas stirred your imagination and welcomed you as the porch was approached. The door to this multi-functional area was a patched screen and had to be quickly opened and closed to keep out the ever-present flies, which would stream in at every opportunity as if conveyed by a powerful vacuum.

The interesting mechanical and medicinal odors of the porch were succeeded by the appetizing smells of the kitchen as one proceeded into this next and most important room. Here was a wood stove, always hot in summer as well as winter. Behind it was a narrow table on which sat one or two pails of fresh milk at just the right temperature to promote the rise to the surface of the delicious cream, which was then made into butter. It was here that I unknowingly entered the cholesterol affair by lapping and sucking up this golden semi-liquid nectar whenever no one was looking. Of course, this questionable conduct left a conspicuous hiatus in the golden circle. And I once apprehensively heard my aunt express her concern about this mystery. Also, back of the wood stove, the medulla oblongata of this wonderful country home, was a wood box full of pine kindling, never anything big and never any hardwood. Perhaps this homogeneous fuel supply allowed an easy regulation of temperature. It was here that chicken was fried in a skillet, rolls were baked to perfection, potatoes and beans were boiled, and brown eggs and pork were fried each morning.

Nearby was a butter churn. At times the children would help in the process, in which agitation would mysteriously turn a liquid into a solid rather than the more rational reverse. The pressing of the butter into a pound or so of cylindrical cakes was my first taste of reproductive casting, an activity that now dominates my life. The press was made of wood with a decorative leaf-like design negatively carved into the top. After pressing, the butter was then removed, wrapped in waxed paper and stored in the zinc-lined wooden icebox where it was kept until set forth on the table at every meal.

In the middle of this eighteen by eighteen foot room was a large round kitchen table, covered with a colorfully decorated oil cloth. All meals were taken here. On special occasions, when friends or relatives were present, additional tables and white linen tablecloths were used.

Of course on a subsistence farm, meals varied with the season. And it is an important added dimension to a meal to have your food not only be a product of your direct efforts but to be the special gift of a season or a certain circumstance. To have the earth circle the sun with its axis inclined on a 22½-degree tilt was a wonderful idea. This simple stratagem cleverly mandates an annual change to what we see, smell, feel, taste and know, and allows us to think of time in a circular and not a linear fashion.

Fried chicken, roasted corn on the cob, soft crabs, strawberries and watermelon were there for one to relish at these special and proper times. It would be productive for the present consumer to compare this mode of living with putting a plastic card on a check-out counter to pay for frozen strawberries, frozen chicken or frozen crabs in January, when one should be properly eating fresh black ducks and oysters. And the converse is equally true.

Connected to the kitchen was a small pantry with a cloth hanging over the entrance. In this culinary deposit box was a wonderful portfolio of jellies, jams and canned (really jarred) beef and pork, neatly lined up on shelves covered with decorated paper. It was, one may muse, an example of man's eternal desire to linger over past pleasures and prepare for the future, as a squirrel stores its acorns.

Now, the negation of the Earth's angled-axis effect by modern air transportation allows one to have fresh vegetables all year round. This shrinking of the world, combined with modern freezing technology, provides a degree of certainty to food availability that may offer some advantage to modern living. However, subsistence farming provided certain delicacies at specific times and gave one something to miss and something to anticipate—two of the most soul-satisfying emotions of man.

On the right-hand side of the pantry between the baseboard and the floor was a mouse hole, and frequently this creature could be seen scurrying to safety when one entered. On the floor in the rear left corner was a metal can with a lid, which in proper circles is referred to as a chamber pot. This was a real luxury when nature called in the middle of a winter night, because there was no plumbing in the house other than the hand pump on the porch.

This description of the times does not mean that this house was lacking in any way. It was a magical, healthy, warm and interesting place to live. That is why I spent as much time there as possible, why I longingly write of it today, and why I would return if I could.

From the kitchen one passed into the living room where there was a tin heater, hand-cranked gramophone, battery-powered radio and the usual couches and chairs. In this room were books and magazines, great attractions for me. My Uncle Melvin read a lot, and western novels by a New York dentist named Zane Grey were abundant. He also subscribed to a magazine devoted to hunting with hounds called *Full Cry*. The Edgar Rice Burroughs' *Tarzan of the Apes* complete series was there and I read them all by oil lamplight.

It was from this library that I borrowed a copy of James Oliver Curwood's *Swift Lightning* in 1943 and coveted it so much and kept it for so long that I became ashamed to return it. It is now one of my most treasured books, despite its dark past.

In this room the progress of World War II was heard every evening, as well as the lighter side of life with Amos and Andy, Jack Benny and all others who made up radio in the early 1940s.

My cousin Melvin, who was always very athletic and competitive, and I devised many indoor games in this room, including ping pong. We did not have a table, we used the floor; we did not have a net, we lined up books with the

112

covers opened slightly for support, and the binding was the top of the net. From the dime store in town, where we went every Saturday night, we each purchased a wooden paddle with a small rubber ball attached to it by means of a two-foot long piece of string-size rubber filament. Thus we had the net, ball and paddle. The decorative squares on the linoleum floor delineated the court, and here we played thousands of games. And I must admit, I never won until my worthy opponent became so bored with my ineptness and lack of improvement that he started to play left-handed for the sake of equality. However, Melvin quickly became so proficient that the handicap disappeared. Finally, our competition ended after a humbling discussion as to the merits of his using a foot. I don't recall whether it was his left or his right, and it doesn't matter anyway.

Continuing aft from this combination gymnasium, reading room, sitting room and music room, there was a hall that led to a staircase and a very formal parlor. I do not recall that this room was ever frequented by adults. Perhaps when folks got together en masse after a funeral, a wedding or a big family convention, someone wandered back there, but normally it was either too hot or too cold. Its only real use, as I recall, was as a cache area for my cousin and me. It was here that we secreted some of our most cherished possessions and our hard-earned money.

Picking strawberries was our favorite pastime, undoubtedly because we were allowed to miss a few days of school for this pleasurable labor. We were paid five cents a quart, and on a good day we might pick sixty or seventy quarts. Also, we sometimes dug potatoes or picked tomatoes, but this was more like work, and we did not have the opportunity to miss school. We kept this money hidden under the couch cushions in a jar or sock. Melvin was the treasurer of his second-grade, an exalted position in my mind, and he had tucked away a jar of pennies and nickels and neatly kept a record of class dues in a composition notebook. Now, over half a century later, he is the accountant and business manager for Turner Sculpture.

Upstairs were two bedrooms, both unheated. A feather mattress was used in the winter in both the adults' and children's rooms. It was sometimes a frigid affair to climb the stairs and go to bed in January or February. And to get up in the middle of the night to answer a call of nature created a classic dilemma—leave the warm bed or let your bladder burst.

For years a barnyard cock roosted in a cottonwood tree next to our bedroom, and every morning around three o'clock he would herald the coming dawn for about ten minutes, then remain silent for the rest of the night. He was there in winter or summer, and even though he was free to use the henhouse, he preferred the Spartan life. They just do not make roosters like that anymore.

In the hallway upstairs was an open stairwell. Here one could lean over the abyss and touch the opposite wall. If he had the strength to push himself back, he would survive. Otherwise, he would certainly perish. Although Melvin-the-acrobat constantly challenged me to imitate his conquering of this maneuver, I never summoned the necessary courage until I was twenty years old and six-foot-one and the house had long since been abandoned.

All windows in this house were of handmade glass. It is now much revered in cabinets because of its inherent imperfections, the same feature that at one time made it obsolete. These defects were bubbles and an uneven surface. The latter creates distorted images, and when very young I would look outside at the flat ground, and it would appear hilly. Immediately I would run out to play on the hills but would, of course, be thwarted. I would repeat this over and over until I was exhausted and quit. I do not know when I became aware of this illusion, nor do I recall when I learned what caused it. But I vividly recall the frustration of not being able to fulfill my fantasy of playing on a hill until I went to the state track meet in Charlottesville.

There was the usual assortment of auxiliary buildings clustered around two sides of the old home: a barn, outhouse, corn crib, hen house, smokehouse and others.

The barn loft was used for hay storage, and some of it was pushed through a small opening to the draft horses below—one of our daily chores. It was also a great place to play and chase pigeons. One day, two holes, each about 4" in diameter, appeared in the tin roof. Two shells from the Navy's target practicing in the Bay had gone astray. Uncle Melvin went into town and telephoned the authorities, and the following day two men came to dig up the unexploded warheads.

The outhouse was a respectable but reachable distance from the home. It was a one-holer, complete with corn cobs and outdated Sears Roebuck and Montgomery Ward catalogues. The latter were not for reading.

I particularly recall the corn stack, filled to its top in the fall with golden ears of corn. Some of these were given to the horses. Others were shelled for the chickens. This was also a chore for the children, and a hand-powered sheller made this an easy job. This machine had a heavy flywheel with a handle attached to it, and some inertia could be accumulated as it was turned faster and faster. My cousin and I would alternate between cranking and putting the corn cobs into an opening on top of the sheller. We made a game of everything that possessed any potential for fun, and one would try to put the corn in so fast that the momentum of the flywheel and the strength of the cranker would be overcome, and the sheller would jam.

Because of my aversion to any kind of dead animal, unless it was on my plate, I vividly recall an unpleasant incident that time has, in its usual way, repainted with humor. On this occasion Melvin was the cranker and I was the stuffer, blindly grabbing ears from the pile as quickly as I could, trying to bring his cranking to a grinding halt. One had to examine each ear to be sure to put the pointed end in first so that the teeth would grab it more easily. Suddenly, in my hands I had not a golden ear of corn, but a fat, dead rat with maggots in its eyeballs. Immediately I dropped it, ran to a nearby horse trough and plunged my hand into the clean water. Actually, I plunged my hand into any water that I could find for a week and ate with my right hand in my pocket for a month.

116

The maintenance of the hen house, as it was feministically called because of the value of eggs and the polygamous capabilities of the rooster, was the sole responsibility of my cousin, and I always offered my assistance whenever I was in residence. We gathered the eggs in a basket, and I would guess that we might get a couple dozen a day, when the laying season was at its peak. These eggs were an important part of the family larder, and we always were careful with them, but one day I broke the entire day's take in a failed scientific experiment, when we decided to investigate centrifugal force. My daring cousin Melvin swung the basket over his head in a complete circle, and the eggs remained in the basket when it was upside down. I felt confident that I could duplicate this feat—it looked so easy. I grabbed the basket, looked at the precious eggs, took a deep breath and, after a few practice oscillations, began the upward swing.

Then suddenly, when the container was at the 11:00 position, the thought came to me that I was toying with breakfast and possibly the Sunday cake. I lost my nerve and aborted the maneuver. The vision of the broken eggs in the path and on the cottonwood roots is still crystal clear, but I have trouble remembering my whereabouts of yesterday.

118

The smokehouse was filled with sugar and salt-coated bacon, hams and shoulders after the fall hog killing. For days a smouldering fire of hickory, cherry and corn cobs slowly preserved the winter's main supply of meat. Often I would open the door and peek at all the swine body parts hanging from the rafters and whet my appetite—pork was my favorite meat until one day I noticed a neat round hole in a ham and a mouse peering out at me.

As it was with most country people, the outdoors was important not only for survival but also recreation. Sunday dinners (noonish) were always, in good weather, followed by a softball game, which included anyone, no matter how young or how old, who desired to play. At times the field hands were summoned to make a complement.

The playing field was shared with a flock of chickens, and on more than one occasion they were downed by a line drive. If seriously injured, they were immediately killed, cleaned and put into the spider.

Like children everywhere in the world, we devised many games of our own. For demographic reasons, most were designed for two people and frequently involved a rubber ball and a bat. One of the most ingenious was played at the rear of the house, which had a tall, brick end. The batter faced the bricks at a distance of about fifteen feet. The pitcher stood behind him and threw the ball against the

119

bricks in such a manner that it bounced back within reach of the batter. The pitcher thus doubled as catcher. The object was to hit the ball so that it again hit the bricks and bounced off. If not caught on the rebound, it was a base hit. If hit hard enough and at the right angle, it would bounce back far enough to go over the wire fence that bordered the cow pasture behind the house. This was a home run, as you probably have guessed.

These bricks at the rear of the house had a conspicuous worn area that represented hundreds of thousands of impacts by rubber balls.

At the other end of the house were similarly worn boards forming the porch. The projectiles in this case were lead BB shot from our air rifles, fired at the innocent flies that soaked up the sun in that area. We became so proficient at this sport that there was actually some danger involved to the flies, but we never made a noticeable dent in their population—just the porch.

From May until September, trips to the swimming hole were frequent, and I recall this activity with the most longing. These occurred at the end of the work day, when we were hot, dirty and tired, and at anytime on the weekend.

The water was, of course, salt. I believe I was fifteen before fresh water ever came above my ankles. The swimming hole was at the mouth of a small inlet that emptied into Craddock Creek, which in turn emptied into the Chesapeake. The bottom here was scoured by the tide and was hard and clean. It was about six feet deep at high tide. Upstream of this inlet, the water broadened out into about twenty shallow acres, full of eel grass, which sheltered the blue crab. Often we would bring along a basket and, with the aid of a stick, catch the big "jimmies," which were plentiful. When the moon was full, we would always find soft crabs taking advantage of the cover while they hardened. They were a welcome addition to the larder.

That was a half-century ago and things have changed. This past summer, Melvin and I were fishing from my outboard skiff in Craddock Creek, and for old time's sake we decided to run over to the old swimming hole where the water was always deep and clear. As we entered the narrow inlet, our motor ran aground even though the tide was up. We got out our paddles and painstakingly retraced our route through the stinking silt that had filled the hole. We will not return and neither will the swimming hole. It has been filled in by years of muddy runoff from greedy farming operations utilizing every inch of land, down to the high-tide mark.

Finally, this homestead was deserted when my relatives bought a farm a few miles away and moved. I frequently went back and wandered through the house, standing, sitting, thinking, imagining, trying to relive. The doors and windows gradually disappeared and the death agony of the old yellow house became evident.

As farming modes changed and land was coveted more and more, this oasis became an obstacle in the middle of one big field. No longer was it the pulsating center of many small fields of different crops necessary to sustain the lives of man and beast. Farmers were no longer content to detour from straight lines, and there were no horses to rest in the shade of the cottonwoods. The death of this place was only a matter of time, and whenever, in my secondhand car, I crossed the threshold from the woods where the blood was in the road, I stopped and looked anxiously at the doomed homeplace. Then the inevitable happened and, when I revisited the old yellow house on a weekend home from college in the early fifties, it was gone. There was nothing left but a pile of black cinders and fallen giant trees with dismembered limbs strewn about awaiting cremation. Wisps of smoke rose from the black ashes. The only recognizable remnants of the house were the bricks that had been the target of countless rubber balls, pieces of broken handmade glass windows and the handle and spout of the hand pump, which had provided a water source for humans and livestock for decades.

As I stood there trying to hear the hounds bark, the rooster crow and the rustle of the cottonwood leaves, a new John Deere tractor plowed ahead in a straight line, preparing the land for a monotonous crop of soybeans destined to be mush or oil for unknown humans in another part of the world. Soon the machine would not be compelled to deviate around the expired home and its once protective cottonwoods. The driver of the tractor looked straight ahead from his enclosed cab. His unweathered, unpatinaed, clammy face showed no feeling for the land, no interest in the swarming gulls nor concern about the coming storm—his expression was as monotonous as a department store mannequin.

Over the Bay, in the northwest, a black cloud materialized and rolled over the field that once was many fields. It came forth just as the bygone thunderstorms that had caused us to drop our hoes or unhook the horses and run for the barn. Its approach was heralded by a foray of dust devils and the refreshing odor of ozone. Then, large precursory drops of rain began to fall, each creating a plaintive sizzle and a gasping breath of steam as it hit the smoldering ashes.

Thunder sounded close by and I counted the seconds, multiplied by one thousand, and estimated the main storm to be at the mouth of Craddock Creek. It was here that I often clammed with Ellis Drummond and my mother and fished for the Speckled trout that patrolled the perimeter of the eel grass beds for soft crabs and minnows. This was before herbicides and pesticides drained from the fields into the Bay and creeks, when the weeds were pulled by hand and before the field hands went north or collected welfare.

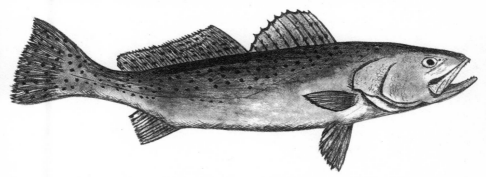

It was beginning to get chilly as the storm front approached, but there was still some residual warmth and comfort from the remains of the house that had sheltered its occupants for a hundred years. I don't know the person who first received the hospitality of this house, but I was surely the last.

It was time to leave, and I got into my car and went out the dirt road, which would soon be obliterated by the tractor and plow. It also had succumbed to progress and had become a path to nowhere and would soon not even be that.

As the road led back into the recently clear-cut woods, I stopped in front of the site of the crumbled tenant house. The ground was damp and the blood should certainly be visible. But it was not there.

Time pushes forward relentlessly, whether it be in a circular or linear fashion, and I was reluctantly being shoved from boyhood into manhood.

PEACOCK PRIDE

It is not the magnitude nor the origin of the inspiration that is important; certainly every avalanche begins with a snowflake somewhere up the mountain.

There is an annual event in Virginia called "Garden Week" in which the hierarchy's homes, some beautiful and some not, are opened to the public. The curious, envious and interested purchase tickets to view these places. The owners make careful preparations in the houses and on the grounds, and in this charitable event each tries to outdo the other. And it is sometimes more conscionable to enjoy your spoils if you allow a few crumbs to benefit fellow humans that got cut short. The ideal way to do this is impersonally, through a charity. In this manner, one does not have to face the misery of the general populace and is not badgered with personal requests for second helpings. This is understandable, and I would certainly prefer making a donation to UNICEF rather than going to the ghettos of Calcutta to personally pass out bread.

Some owners of these homes on the local tour considered themselves a wee bit better than the regular

125

Eastern Shore of Virginia subspecies. Possibly they were justified in this assumption because, for one reason or another, they sure had a lot more stuff. And frequently artisans and craftsmen were imported from cities up north to perform certain jobs that could just as easily be bungled by local folks who needed the money.

One year, I think it was about 1950, I was involved in helping with the decor of one of these beautiful mansions. It all began when a peacock was accidentally electrocuted, and the mistress of the house decided to have this bird mounted for display on the coming tour.

A phone call was made to Robert Rockwell, my friend and mentor, who was probably the world's foremost taxidermist. However, Mr. Rockwell was retired and did not want to take on this job. He suggested that I be contacted. Of course, I needed the money, but twenty-five dollars was as much as they would pay. Still, I would have settled for less, because I felt honored to be asked to prepare the peacock and to play even a minor part in redistributing wealth and ridding the world of poverty.

My mother drove me to this mansion, about thirty miles away, to pick up the unfortunate bird. The long and beautiful driveway led to a magnificent home replete with a butler standing smartly at attention by the front entrance. We stopped here and I was directed to the rear. My mother waited in the car, and I went into a huge kitchen in which there were several black servants. I vividly recall two of these, the cook and the chauffeur. The latter wore a tailored uniform that was black with a gray shirt and a black bow tie. His aquiline features reminded one of a Greek god with a neatly trimmed moustache. I sensed he was a person of authority and envied his station in life. Certainly, with further exposure, he would have become a role model. But in that fleeting contact, he was at least inspiring. It is not the magnitude nor the origin of the inspiration that is important; certainly every avalanche begins with a snowflake somewhere up the mountain.

The fat cook was attractive in her own way. She had a bright smile with a full complement of perfect teeth. Although she was busy preparing a delicate souffle or something of that nature, I felt that her real forte was one of my favorites—turnip greens and chitlings.

Both of these humans would make proper impressions as their lives brushed with those of so-called "attractive" people. Additionally, they both impressed me, but I never saw either again.

I particularly recall the conversation I overheard between these striking servants. The cook said, "What do you want for breakfast, James ?" He replied, "I'll have a steak." Whereupon she opened the door of a huge refrigerator and brought forth a piece of meat three inches thick and about the size of a tomato basket lid. I had always wanted a steak, and immediately I made it a goal to someday own a piece of meat like James'. This lesson was perhaps more valuable than the twenty-five dollars.

The male peacock was taken from a freezer and presented to me by the gardener, who had a very British accent. Along with the bird I was given some instructions in a dubious and patronizing manner. It was apparent that he had no confidence in ordinary colonials.

The bird was a good specimen with a long trail of "eyed" scapular feathers, which most people erroneously call its tail. There was not a blemish on this bird, and I was eager to restore it to life.

We returned home, my mother proud of my presumed ability, while I was contemplating how I was to go about this important commission. Although under Mr. Rockwell's guidance I had mounted a few ducks that were satisfactory, I had some reservations as to whether I could please the owners of this mansion with my mounting of their peacock. Perhaps that big steak had an influence on my thinking.

I took the bird out back to my father's workshop as soon as it thawed out and began work. Two days of tedium were required for its reconstruction, and Mr. Rockwell stopped by when I was finished. He seemed pleased, and the only suggestion he made was to twist the head to one side slightly for some asymmetry. "Don't make any hood ornaments," was his gift to me on that day. Knowing he meant this to apply to sculpture as well, I have not forgotten. The mounted bird was allowed to dry for two weeks with its long train of blue, green and gold feathers supported from the ceiling.

When the project was finished, a truck was sent to pick up the bird, its spread of feathers being too great for a car. I had completed this task just in time for Garden Tour, as promised.

My boon companion, Mitt Bundick, was a rough old outdoorsman who scoffed at the finer things of life. However, his wife Blanche was a very genteel lady who dearly loved the annual garden tour. She knew I had mounted a peacock for one of the homes on the tour, and she hoped to see it displayed. Mrs. Bundick was among a group of about twenty people as they were led into a huge glass-enclosed room with a pool and gardens. The guide explained the magic of the room with its controls for light and humidity, then focused her attention on my mounted peacock, conspicuously displayed near flowers.

"This peacock," she told the group, "was especially mounted by a famous taxidermist from Philadelphia, and the cost was five-hundred dollars."

Everyone was deeply impressed, and as they looked at this creature with their jaws agape, a voice piped up from the group.

"Well, that is not so—Billy Turner did that, and he only got twenty-five dollars."

The articulate hostess made no comment but hurried the

group along to see the next marvel. Blanche wasn't convinced that she had made her point, so later that day she fell in with another group and took the tour again. As she expected, it was again repeated that the bird had been stuffed by the world famous bird stuffer from Philadelphia. Blanche again set the hostess straight and this time felt that she was making headway.

Just to be sure, Blanche returned on the next day to take the tour for the third time. The guide looked the group over carefully, called attention to the stuffed peacock and said, "This bird was prepared for exhibit by our own Billy Turner from Belle Haven."

SWEETHEART AND CABELL

. . . he enjoyed playing jokes on just about anyone except very recent widows, severe cripples and retarded babies. . .

Cabell Mapp, my mentor and neighbor, loved to tease and joke and was a true expert at both. He was not a spontaneous pie-in-the-face type, but planned and schemed for a predictable outcome. Actually, I think he savored the planning stage as much as the execution. The masterpiece that I will now relate is a classic example of his ability to seize an opportunity for subtle amusement and nourish and guide the ensuing drama as predictably as a New York playwright.

Being somewhat of a game-law violator, Cabell naturally was the target of local game wardens, but this did not bother him—he loved to be the prey as much as the predator. And while he enjoyed playing jokes on just about anyone except very recent widows, severe cripples and retarded babies, people in authority were his favorite target. I think he thought of his pranks as a public service to keep officials on their toes.

131

Sweetheart Charnock[4] was one of his favorite wardens for tantalization, and I'll give you an example of their lifelong cat-and-mouse game, which I believe they both enjoyed.

One day Cabell was in the local drug store in Belle Haven, a place where cronies congregated, and saw Sweetheart park his truck out front. The warden usually dropped in once or twice a week for a vanilla milkshake, although it was well known that this was not his favorite beverage. No one knows how long Cabell had been planning this prank. Some say he was in the store knowing that Sweetheart was in the vicinity and was apt to stop by. Others say it all came to him when the warden's truck came to a halt, and Cabell saw him through the gilded glass store window.

Timing is of the essence in many things of importance, such as hooking a fish or shooting a partridge, but nowhere is it more so than in a joke. At this, Cabell was a master. As Sweetheart opened the door to the drugstore, Cabell, who had already turned his back, began in mid-sentence, " . . . and my dog pointed four coveys of birds, and I shot ten of them and only missed. . ." and he stopped talking just as his eyes caught Sweetheart's. He put on a "caught-in-the-act" act and quickly grabbed his milkshake and sucked on the double straws until they made a gurgling, slurping sound, as the level of the liquid reached the bottom. He

---

[4] A name which certainly needs an explanation—Sweetheart was a nickname for this old game warden because that and "Honey" were the only ways he ever addressed anyone.

was desperately pretending to be desperately pretending. Right away it was very plain to Sweetheart that Cabell was just faking a nonchalant innocent attitude and had been caught in bragging on shooting quail out of season. Of course, Sweetheart couldn't arrest Cabell without catching him in the act of committing a game-law violation or obtaining a confession. Both of these possibilities were very remote, but naturally Sweetheart tried right away to pursue the latter. "Cabell," he said, "keep right on and finish your tale." Cabell, of course, was ready for this and said, "Sure, I'll continue—you see, Sweetheart, I was just sitting here telling a tale my grandad told me about shooting birds one day about twenty years ago, and as I was saying, my grandad said, 'I was down on the Somers' farm and my dog pointed four coveys of birds and I shot ten of them and only missed one and it was out of season and the damned game warden didn't catch me,' that's what grandad told me." Then he vacuumed the bottom of the milk shake glass a little more, feigning nervousness.

Cabell knew that Sweetheart would know that there had been a generation switch, and this was just part of the aggravation Cabell delightedly injected into the whole charade.

Sweetheart was as mad as he could be at this flaunting of the law, but he knew he would have to bide his time. "Well, Honey," he said, "I'm going to get you one of these days." And he meant it. Cabell was pleased to hear this because he was in the middle of the doldrums between the end of the hunting season and the beginning of the fishing season, and he desperately needed some sport to fill this seasonal hiatus.

Now here in Act Two, about a week later, we find Cabell on the phone with Sweetheart's wife. "Mrs. Charnock, I can't tell you who this is, but will you tell Sweetheart that Cabell Mapp is going to be down on the Somers' farm tomorrow morning shooting birds?" She, of course, agreed to do this because, like all good wives, she took an interest in her husband's career and supported him in any way she could.

It was, of course, legal at any time of the year to train your dogs without shooting. Cabell did this between seasons and now was planning to get in some post-season training while having fun with Sweetheart at the same time.

The next morning Cabell donned his bloody old gunning coat and loaded his bird dogs into his truck. I met him as he had requested because I knew something big was in the wind. In his coat were five big sweet potatoes and a package of Chinese firecrackers, a bottle of whiskey, a pocket knife and a ball of twine—all carefully chosen props for the final act. We drove down Occohannock Neck, turned off into the woods road that entered the Somers' place and parked the truck conspicuously beside a field.

Cabell knew that somewhere out in the woods or brush he was being watched by Sweetheart. First, the warden had to be located without his knowing. In order for the trick to work properly, it was essential that Cabell be caught in the act at somewhat of a distance. He knew the warden was watching his every move, although he didn't know exactly from where. But Cabell knew how to make his opponent "blow his cover."

He let his dogs out and reached for the bottle of whiskey. In as conspicuous a manner as possible, and on one side of the truck, Cabell took a swig. Then he walked around to the other side, kicked at the exposed tire fabric on that side and took another drink. Having laid the ground work, he set the bottle on the hood. Cabell knew that there were two things that pleased Sweetheart. One was a drink of whiskey, and the other was catching a game-law violator.

Now the trap was set, and Cabell walked on across the unplowed corn field with the two pointers in front and me trailing behind with an empty potato sack. We all disappeared into the brush on the other side of the field. I held the dogs, and Cabell crawled back to watch the truck.

It didn't take long for Sweetheart to come out of the bushes not far from the truck and casually stroll toward it. Cautiously, he walked toward the cab and paused within reach of the bottle. Satisfied that no one was looking, he grabbed the bottle and unscrewed the cap. Wiping the mouth, and still looking in every direction, he took a quick but ample draught. Gentleman that he was, Sweetheart again wiped the mouth of the bottle and replaced its cap. Cabell was impressed by this gesture.

Now, having established Sweetheart's whereabouts, the next phase of the operation began. We came out into the open field, and Sweetheart ducked behind the front tire of Cabell's truck.

Cabell had let Sweetheart know where we were, while

at the same time letting the warden think that he had not been spotted. All systems were go.

There were several coveys of birds on the Somers' place, and we knew their habits pretty well from the season just passed. We went into a cut over woods and kept close to the edge so our movements were plainly visible to the warden.

Cabell had cut a stick and tied one of the firecrackers to the small end and when Oreo, his brown and white pointer, found a covey, he touched his Lucky Strike to the fuse and flushed the birds. The timing was perfect; the birds jumped, Cabell tossed a potato into the air, and the firecracker exploded as he held the stick to his shoulder. I ran ahead and pretended to pick up a bird, which was a potato, and put it into the sack. Sweetheart took ad-vantage of our distraction to close the gap to 50 yards, stopped, and hid behind a big pine stump.

We worked the singles and Cabell soon had about five birds or—more accurately—five potatoes. He even missed a few, and we both cursed loud enough for Sweetheart to hear. Even Cabell missed once in a while, and we wanted everything to be authentic.

Sweetheart was now within striking distance, so we sat down to let him make his *coup de grâce*. We could hear him creeping up on us, and it was very difficult to keep from laughing.

When he was close, Cabell heard him and told me to "run for it." We both took off. It was pretty clear that the whiskey was beginning to get to Sweetheart, and he couldn't keep up the pace. So Cabell got tangled up in some bull briars and, while desperately calling for me to help him, allowed himself to be caught. I was so absorbed with the reality of the act that I forgot I was innocent. I had done some real running from wardens before because of Cabell's bad influence, and it all came natural.

Cabell called out to me, "Come back, Billy, and bring the sack. I've been caught."

I realized that Cabell always liked an audience of some kind, even if it was just the dogs and me, so I returned. Actually, I wanted to see the showdown.

Sweetheart was really gloating over his catch, and Cabell shed a tear knowing that he was in for a big fine.

The interrogation went something like this:

"Well, Cabell, how many birds did you kill?"

"Why, I didn't shoot any birds."

"Where's your gun? I'm going to take it for evidence."

"I don't have no gun, Sweetheart."

"You've hid it, so you give it to me or leave it here to rust. I see the birds in the sack—give them to me." (Sweetheart had been accused before of eating the evidence.)

Cabell reaffirmed he had no birds, so Sweetheart put his hand into the sack and retrieved, one by one, five potatoes. He still refused to believe that we were not criminals (actually we were), so Cabell lit a firecracker and threw it at the ground and both of us burst out laughing.

Sweetheart tried to salvage something and threatened to charge us with masquerading, flaunting, escaping or a dozen other things when Cabell brought it all to an end with a legal observation of his own.

"Sweetheart, you stole my whiskey and you're drinking on the job."

Sweetheart mulled this over for a spell then turned away. As he walked by Cabell's truck he paused, looked at the bottle of whiskey on the hood, then kept on going.

One day a couple of months later, Cabell and I were out at the mouth of Occohannock Creek shad fishing with nets. Shad are the first fish available in the spring, when they seek out brackish or fresh water for spawning. They are full of very fine bones, and if one can avoid these, the meat is delicious. Their roe is, however, the real delicacy. When scrambled up with gull eggs, you cannot find a better breakfast. Of course, gull egging is illegal, but somehow Cabell and I would always find some each spring. Anyway, we were running out our net when a fellow fisherman stopped by for a gab. After discussing the fishing situation, he mentioned that Sweetheart had died that morning. This was, for both of us, sad news. Cabell immediately pulled in our net without saying a word, and we went on back to the dock. I had known Sweetheart only a short time, but Cabell had been on the run from him for about thirty years. He was obviously shaken by the death of a man that most people considered to be Cabell's worst enemy.

A couple of days later, Cabell and I went down to the funeral home to pay our last respects. As we were standing beside the open casket thinking about times past and times that would never be, Cabell reached into his pocket for something. I had thought it was a handkerchief because of the tears trickling down his cheeks. But it was not. In his hand were a few Bobwhite quail feathers. He placed them beside Sweetheart, and we left. An era was over, and poaching would never be the same.

THE LAST PICNIC

*We toted all of our jelly beans, candy bars, ginger snaps and honey buns
back into the woods to this beautiful and sacred spot for the annual feast.*

My cousin, Melvin, and I were deeply religious
children. We faithfully celebrated Easter every year with a
picnic back in the woods on the shores of Craddock Creek,
the most important body of water in our world. In
preparation for this we would save our money from the sale
of scavenged pop bottles and eggs all during the winter so
we could purchase enough food for our annual ritual. There
was no ham, beans or even bread on our menu, only sinfully
sweet candy and pastries of every shape, size, color and
taste.

Of course, the setting is what makes a picnic, otherwise
one could just stay at home and sit in a chair at a table and
not have to contend with bugs, weather or other
unforeseeable inconveniences. The poorest fare in the
proper setting becomes a feast, but it seems that the older I
get the more the opposite of this becomes true.

The path to our picnic site had for years wound through

a beautiful forest of loblolly pines, which I imagined were as big as the redwoods I would not see until thirty years later. There was no underbrush in these woods. A herd of semi-wild goats took care of the bull briars, poison ivy and other undergrowth. The result was a whispering canopy of green supported by hundreds of tall swaying columns arising from a soft brown carpet of pine shatters[5].

Our forest, however, had been timbered a few months prior to the story I am telling, and except for a huge pile of sawdust, all that remained were fallen limbs, stumps and scattered hardwoods. In those days the logs were sawed on the spot by a semi-portable sawmill, and only the rough lumber was hauled away. Our path to the picnic grounds and the swimming hole led by the sawdust, and we stopped here this chilly April Sunday to feel the magical warmth of the spontaneous combustion, which could burn your skin if you dug deeply enough into the mountain of decaying cellulose. We were heavily laden with our sweet repast and heading for the official picnic site on the creek shore at the mouth of a small cove and not far from the Chesapeake.

Here the water was about fifty feet wide, and the ebb and flow of the tide kept it scoured out to about five or six feet at high tide, an ideal depth for swimming. Every hot afternoon in the summer would find my cousins and our field-hand friends cooling off at this delightful spot. We would dive for shells and marvel at how well sound traveled under water when two clams were tapped together. After a

---

[5] Needles of the loblolly pine.

swim we would quickly fill a bushel basket with blue crabs, abundant in the shallow cove. We did not use a net to catch them—we simply pinned them to the soft bottom with a forked stick and, after the mud cleared, carefully picked them up by a back fin. We also would pick up a few bull tongue oysters when my aunt requested.

This was the general area for our picnic. The specific spot where we spread our table cloth—actually a horse blanket—was a mound of earth and bricks on the bank, which we knew for certain was an Indian gravesite. On the horizon was the Chesapeake Bay and the limits of the world.

I remember our final picnic in particular. We toted all of our jelly beans, candy bars, ginger snaps and honey buns back into the woods to this beautiful and sacred spot for the annual feast. Nearly there, we remembered our Pepsi-Colas were left behind. So it was agreed that Melvin, being fleet of foot, would go back to the house to pick up our beverages. His parting words to me, being one year my senior, were "Billy, you stay and watch this food, and I'll be back with the drinks real quick!"

I agreed to abide by my senior's instructions, and he went off through the woods, back to his mother's ice box for our drinks. Patience was never one of my virtues, and he had not been gone long when I became a little uneasy. Compounding my uneasiness was the idea we had encamped on an Indian burial ground. So, probably about the time he had arrived back at the house, I had decided to leave my post and meet Melvin halfway—enough sitting in the woods on Indian graves all by myself!

I retraced our tracks down the path and had gone only about a quarter-mile when I met Melvin returning with the two Pepsi-Colas. The first thing he did was to reprimand me for abandoning my post. I pointed out to him that I saw no need to stand guard, because nothing was going to get our picnic. Nevertheless, he was a bit put out that I had not obeyed his orders, and I was a little ruffled that he had dressed me down. However, it was Easter, and peace and good will were in the air, so we hurried back toward the picnic site to begin our gluttony.

We had not gone far when we heard something that sounded like a pack of hounds at a 'coon kill right at its peak, combined with a bunch of hogs on slop. Melvin became suspicious that our picnic was proceeding without us. We raced to the area and, as we approached the bank, saw six hound-dog tails wagging in the air above the bayberry bushes. We rushed to the rescue, but our food was almost gone. Old Tray, my uncle's favorite coonhound, and I made a dive at the same time for a big chocolate rabbit, which, other than a few jellybeans and part of a licorice stick, was all that remained of our Easter feast. Not only did Tray beat me to the bunny, but he ate one of the last jellybeans. I let Melvin have the licorice stick, and I took the meager remains.

We drank the two Pepsis, enjoyed the view, and then all eight of us went home, some with full bellies and some empty.

We had performed this rite on many occasions, but things were changing. Melvin had a few black hairs in his armpits, and my voice was beginning to vary in pitch. It was becoming time for hay rides, hot dog roasts and activities in which the other sex would play, at least initially, a minor part.

When customs or lives have run their natural course, it often takes only a small incident to deliver the final blow. So it was with our annual Easter picnic.

THE SPIRIT OF AN OTTER

. . . I was now an accomplice and subject to Mitt's orders but was relieved to a degree when he said, "We are going to take him alive— if he don't eat us up in the meantime."

"Do you want a Coke?" Mitt asked as I stepped out of my father's pick-up. Mitt Bundick always began and ended every expedition with a Coca-Cola. He purchased them by the case in the standard size green glass bottles. Had he been stranded for days in the desert without water, he would not have drunk his favorite beverage from a metal can.

"No," I answered, "it's too cold for me to drink a Coke—how about a cup of Blanche's hot chocolate?"

"We ain't got time. The tide won't wait for us," he explained as he packed his pipe with the nub of his right index finger, all that remained from a childhood hunting accident. I didn't question his decision—from my years with Mitt, I knew he usually was right. He had lived from nature his entire life and had developed an insight into the outdoors, evident in his every move and every word. His sinewy, weather-beaten appearance was the physical confirmation of his livelihood and his passion for nature.

145

My introduction to this 65-year-old purveyor of death and captivity to wildlife of every form that had the slightest potential for profit began with racoon hunting with my Uncle Melvin. I, too, loved the chase and the baying of the hounds, and the ensuing live capture of the prey appealed to me. Actually, I considered myself somewhat of a humanitarian, because my job was to put a specially-altered nail keg over the racoon after my uncle shook it from a tree into the maws of a half-dozen black and tan 'coon hounds. My agility in those days meant that no sooner had the racoon hit the ground than I had it under the keg, and on many occasions I caught the 'coon in mid-air. These live racoons were taken to Mitt, who sold them for restocking in other areas less populated with these fortunate or perhaps unfortunate animals.

Mitt also live-trapped racoons and squirrels for sale to anyone who would answer his ads in the outdoor magazines. You may say he franchised me, since he showed me how to build and set these box traps and purchased all my captives. Our business relationship eventually turned to friendship, and we spent considerable time together enjoying the outdoors.

On this day I was home from college for a weekend and was looking forward to a morning in the field with my companion of the woods and marshes of the Eastern Shore. We threw some rope, steel traps and sacks into the back of his truck, crossed the railroad track and headed for Occohannock Creek, a tidal inlet emptying into the Chesapeake.

146

There are several of these creeks on the Bay side of the peninsula, and most have a marsh or swamp of a few acres at their source. In these marshes, the inlets narrow to a few yards and meander snake-fashion, gradually becoming smaller and more brackish until they evolve into a freshlet and then a ditch. And with this change in habitat comes a change in the wildlife, especially in the marine life.

This was our general destination as we started down the Bayside road in a cab filled with smoke from Mitt's pipe. On these excursions, I had long ago learned to always expect Mitt to come up with a bit of philosophy or wisdom whenever the circumstances allowed. And we had not gone far when he stopped his truck to pick up a potato sack lying in the middle of the road.

"Bill," he said, "there's always a use for a good sack, and they cost a dime if you buy them. You can put a racoon in one, but it had better be new. Older ones are good to dry beans or squash."

He added this sack to the paraphernalia in the back of our truck and continued commenting on other uses for them, such as net storage, rugs and camouflage for duck blinds. Then he stopped again to pick up a stick of wood that he claimed would save him 1¢ on his heating bill. The theory was interesting, but I suspected that he may have lost 2¢ in gas with the braking and accelerating. We had gone only a quarter of a mile when he halted to pick up a road-killed rabbit that would help feed his penned-up racoons. Getting tired of stopping and starting, I reminded him of the tide, so he decided to scavenge on the way back.

We soon approached the town of Pennyville. Mitt pointed the stem of his pipe to a white bungalow with smoke curling from its chimney and a neat woodpile beside it and said, "I got in trouble there about a week ago." The place looked innocent to me, but as was expected of me, I asked, "How did that happen?"

"Well, that's where Sarah Jo bootlegs whiskey by the drink. She charges $1.00 per shot, but she's good to look at, and I stop by once in a while because Blanche don't like me to drink around the house."

He paused as he beat his pipe on the rear-view mirror, then resumed, "I was supposed to be 'coon hunting with your uncle, but when the dogs headed out into Dahl's Swamp, I decided to take a break and visit Sarah Jo. I was sitting by that window sipping my whiskey," he said as he leaned over to get a better look as we drove by.

"See those broken window panes—Blanche did that," he explained. "I was just finishing my drink when a chunk of fire wood come right through the window."

He winced as he re-experienced this near disaster and continued, "I thought I had been shot until Blanche stuck her head through the broken window and told me to come home. And you know Blanche, so I did what she said."

We soon turned off the macadam onto a field road that led through a cutover woods and came to a halt next to the shores of the headwaters of Occohannock Creek. Tied to a tree was a wooden boat.

As we stepped out of the truck, a cranky (great blue heron) uttered a cry that plainly was a combination of alarm

148

and disgust.

"He don't want us in his territory" Mitt explained to me.

"You think he's the same one we always see here?" I queried the ultimate authority.

"Yeah, and he's probably the same one that was here last year—they got their favorite fishing spots just like you and me."

And suddenly the discussion took on a character not so closely resembling that of birdwatchers as Mitt reminisced "When I was a kid we had cranky for supper nearly every Sunday."

Our ornithological discussion terminated with Mitt's favorite heron recipe and his welcome statement: "I don't eat 'em anymore, I got tired of them growing up."

I transferred our equipment from truck to boat and we slid it down the mud incline until it was floating. "Let's check the net first," Mitt suggested.

He had set this net the night before. It was a short net—just enough to go across the narrow body of water. As the beginning flood tide caught the skiff and began to carry us in the direction of the net, Mitt poled along with his pipe in his mouth. Despite his outdoor aptitude, I do not believe he knew how to row, paddle or skull. But his activities never carried him far from shore and a sapling with the knots smoothed off was ample for all his needs. He never tired regardless of the weather, terrain or duration of the voyage.

"Grab that brail, Bill," Mitt requested, then added,

"We'll let the tide keep the stern off the net." We drifted with the tide until the net came up semi-taut.

We pulled the net onto the stern, knowing we had some fish because the corks were bobbing and we could feel their futile struggles. It was getting late in the season for trapping, but it was still early for fish, so this was not a serious and pure attempt at fishing. "Just filling in," Mitt called it.

The gut across which Mitt had set the net was bordered by a combination of saltwater spartina and freshwater cattails. As one came closer to the source, the marshland increased and the channel narrowed. The water was deep in places despite its narrowness, and on low tide huge and ancient cypress stumps came close to the surface. But there are no cypress trees in this area now, and I suppose the rising water levels of past centuries had destroyed an arboreal fairyland long before the first settlers came.

The net contained an interesting catch—two muskrats were entangled in the meshes along with four species of fresh and saltwater fish. These were black bass and bluegills of the former category, and mullet and striped bass of the latter. The black bass and bluegills develop wanderlust in the spring and migrate toward the saltwater. The striped bass are cold-water fish, and the mullet had failed to migrate the previous fall and were now large—some weighing three pounds.

"We got to check the muskrat traps before the tide gets

up," Mitt emphasized. These traps are set in the leeds[6] at low tide so you can see the holes and paths and are more easily checked when the water is low.

The sun was getting up close to the trees now, and the warmth and sun stirred the emotions of a few early red-winged blackbirds staking out their nesting territory in the cattails. A kingfisher rattled its cry, unseen around a bend.

Mitt paused in his poling, repacked his pipe and mused, "I think I'm going to get him today."

"Him" in this case was his favorite adversary, the otter. I did not like the thought of trapping these beautiful, entertaining weasels of the wetlands, but I enjoyed the outdoors and Mitt's company, and my rationale was that he would do it anyway.

Mitt had made three sets for otter—each a series of four foot traps placed as inconspicuously as possible in their paths, which were obvious because of the mud and their habit of sliding down banks.

"Nothing here," Mitt muttered as we approached the first set, so cleverly concealed that I could not see it except for a pole driven into the mud.

We left it undisturbed and continued on to the next set, where the channel had almost doubled back on itself, making a natural shortcut across the intervening marsh for an otter traveling by water. It was here on an isthmus 8-10 feet wide that Mitt had made his most optimistic set.

"Look at those torn-up cattails," Mitt excitedly

---

[6] A path leading to a muskrat's underground home.

exclaimed as we approached. The area looked as if someone had been there with a huge lawnmower—all plant life had been cut off even with the ground and chewed up. But nowhere could I see an otter. Mitt was confident, however. "Take the axe and cut two forked saplings," he told me as he pushed his pole into the mud for an anchor.

"I see him," Mitt hollered as he put his pipe away and untangled some rope.

I soon approached with the saplings, and suddenly, with a clanging of metal, a huge otter charged us. Instantly my admiration of his beauty and courage made me wish that he would escape. I was now an accomplice and subject to Mitt's orders but was relieved to a degree when he said, "We are going to take him alive—if he don't eat us up in the meantime."

Mitt pondered aloud a battle plan for a few moments, then decided that each of us would pin down one end of the otter with the forked saplings, take off the leg traps and ease him into a sack. But the otter was quick as well as angry and he grabbed the saplings with his teeth and almost tore them away as we sparred for an opportunity to pin him to the ground.

It was a long, hard-fought battle, and I will not give a blow by blow account. I will say that at times Mitt was so muddy it was difficult to distinguish him from the otter, and the vantage shifted several times. In the end, however, with the aid of nooses, ropes and bags, we subdued our worthy adversary. He was shoved into a bag, which was then placed in another. The traps were removed from his legs.

"Let's check the next trap," Mitt said, and we poled across the creek to an irrigation dam where there was a slide.

As we approached, Mitt seemed relieved: "We don't have one here."

We returned to the landing and put the otter into the back of the truck, tied the bag to the railing so he wouldn't roll off and headed home. It is surprising how an animal can travel in a sack. I recall once when 'coon hunting with Uncle Melvin and Mitt that we lost two sacks of racoons. There were two in each sack, and these were tied together. We had not finished hunting for the day, so we left them at the base of a big "home" tree. When we returned about two hours later, the sacks were gone. Since then, we have wisely tied the sacks to a bush or limb.

We took the same route home and stopped to pick up a pop bottle from a ditch. Mitt took advantage of this pause to re-light his pipe, and between the start-up puffs said, "Bill, you see this ditch, well I've seen the time it was full of little fish of all colors." I thought about this and replied, "I don't see how any fish can be in that dried up ditch."

"I've seen 'em many a time," he replied in a slightly irritated way.

I didn't believe him, and since I'd had a semester of college biology, I knew I was right.

When we got back to Mitt's headquarters, an assortment of shacks, cages and pens in his backyard, we took the otter off the back of the truck. As Mitt opened a Coke and gave me one, he thought aloud and said, "What in the hell am I going to do with this thing?" He loaded his pipe then added, "He'll go right through every pen I got."

"Well Mitt, we better get him in something because he's gnawing a hole in the bags."

"Roll that 50-gallon drum up here. I'll keep him there until I can build a pen."

I obeyed while Mitt finished his Coke and played with Popeye, his stud "rat terrier," really just a small mongrel with his tail chopped off. Actually, Mitt had developed his personal breed and Popeye kept his harem of about six bitches always with pups, which were sold to the unsuspecting. "Every bit helps" was Mitt's philosophy.

We took the bag out of the bag and put it most of the way into the oil drum.

"You put the top on and hold it tight as soon as the bag comes out," Mitt ordered.

I was hoping that the otter would escape at this point but performed my job as Mitt sliced the bag, letting the otter fall to the bottom of the drum, then quickly pulling out the bag.

We piled some bricks, a busted commode and a plow point on the lid of the container. At first there was a silence, but this was soon followed by an explosion of energy and frenzy in the barrel as the creature attempted to escape. The sound of claws scraping on the metal were combined with snarls and coughs, which plainly showed that our captive was unhappy. I was unhappy also.

"You come back tomorrow and we'll build a pen," Mitt said as I left. It was getting late, and I wanted to go bullfrogging that evening, so I hurried away.

The next morning I arrived to help Mitt build a pen, and the first thing I noticed was the activity in the barrel had become less evident.

"He kept me up all night hollering and clawing," Mitt complained as he opened up his morning Coke.

We started constructing the pen, and it took us until noon to do the job. I didn't mind because Mitt always paid me well for any kind of construction. By the time we finished, the noise in the barrel had ceased. Before we transferred the otter to the pen, Mitt decided to pay me for my labor. This was done in his usual way as each of us sat on a basket to take a break and drink a Coke. He took out his billfold, which was always thick, and began throwing dollar bills on the ground.

"Is that enough?," he paused.

"Sure Mitt, that's fine."

"Well, have two more."

"Thanks Mitt. Now, let's transfer this otter."

We walked over to the quiet barrel, expecting to hear a protecting snarl, but there was no challenge. Mitt kicked the barrel. "I'll wake him up."

But there was no reply.

Carefully, Mitt eased back the lid and peeped in. "Give me that stick Bill," he said, and I handed him a slender butter-bean pole. He poked at the unseen beast in the bottom of the can.

Not getting any response, he continued to slide the lid back and peered in.

"Bill, this otter is dead."

Suddenly I felt as if I were an accomplice to a murder.

Mitt reached in and grabbed the weasel by the tail, lifting it out.

"Look at those toenails," he pointed out with his pipe.

The toenails were mere bleeding stubs, and the inside of the once rusty can was polished as bright and smooth as a mirror.

Mitt had taken out his knife and was honing it on a brick as he explained, "I could have got $50 for him alive. Now, I'll only get $15 for his skin."

So it was with Mitt's economics.

A few years ago, thirty years after this incident and ten after Mitt's death, I was jogging beside a ditch now full of water but dry a week before. The water merely collected in this shallow trench—there was no ingress or egress. It would fill after a rain, then soon dry up.

By habit, I always look at water surfaces, whenever the opportunity is there, and this morning I thought I caught a quick movement below the scum and plastic bottles as I jogged along. I stopped and got down on hands and knees and, after waiting a few moments, a small fish came to the surface to absorb some heat from the early April sun as frogs sang their courting songs from a thousand niches. Soon came another movement under a floating oak leaf. I hastily returned to my studio and came back with a butterfly net. I made several passes at these elusive fish and finally caught about six. They were placed in a pickle jar and their brilliant colors became apparent. They had yellows, reds, blues and greens on their inch-and-a-half long bodies and were two distinct species—one with a spoon-shaped tail and rounded head. The other had a forked tail and an arrow shaped head.

The colored minnows circling the perimeter of this jar trying to escape from their temporary confinement reminded me of Mitt and his otter. I stood by the polluted ditch trying to imagine how a man could eat herons and kill an otter, yet know and admire these delicate fish, which I had not believed existed.

THE FINAL CROSSING

*But age and its consequences were slowly channeling him into a chute,
leaving few choices in the time remaining.*

After my freshman year at the University of Virginia in
Charlottesville, a friend and I decided to seek employment
on the Chesapeake Bay ferries.

The geographical nature of the Eastern Shore of
Virginia, the peninsula that forms the eastern boundary for
the southern portion of the Bay, has for centuries
necessitated marine transportation for connection to the rest
of the state. The proximity of the tip of the peninsula to
metropolitan Hampton Roads has made this area one of the
main points of embarkation and debarkation. During most
of the first half of the twentieth century there has been a
scheduled crossing of the mouth of the Bay with a motor-
propelled ferry, either steam or diesel.

Working on the ferries appealed to us for several
reasons. To begin with, we desperately needed money.
More importantly, the work schedule was two days on and
two off. This would allow me to continue my boat-building

160

business, which still offered some opportunities, but was on the wane due to the increasing popularity of factory-made craft. And we thought that manual labor and the salt air would be a good change from the pseudo-intellectualism that had been such an overpowering influence on us during the past nine months.

In early June of 1954, we caught the ferry at Kiptopeke and went to the headquarters on the Western Shore, intending to apply for jobs as deck hands, although we were certainly capable of being a captain or at least a first mate. It was just that being a deck hand required no Coast Guard license and would give us a chance to see how the rest of the world struggled to survive without a year of college.

After disembarking, we went to the first office we saw and told the woman in attendance that we would like to apply for a job. She took us in to see the boss. He was a blonde, small, young man with a peculiarly northern city accent, and he wore suspenders, a bow tie and a pin-striped shirt—not exactly my idea of a sea captain. His name was Solomon Goldberg. He seemed impressed with our college backgrounds and evidently had never heard of the wild escapades that had been a part of our high school years. We were immediately hired, and he was always a good and fair boss.

It turned out that we were to be hired as stewards and would work for the concessionaire, the Union News Company of Philadelphia, and not be employed by the ferry organization as able-bodied seamen. Every summer the traffic increased, and we applied at the time an additional ferry was being put on full-time to cope with this annual fluctuation of business. Stewarding was actually a much better job than being a deck hand. It was cleaner, less strenuous and more lucrative.

Our duty as stewards was to man the concession, which sold soft drinks, candy, cigarettes and, lastly and mainly, beer. Sailors especially purchased a lot of beer. The price was about twice that on shore, but the young servicemen going to and coming from the Naval Base in Norfolk did not object, and they could not patronize a competitor.

One had the opportunity to observe all forms of humanity while "tending the store" on the Chesapeake Bay ferries. Besides the sailors, there were rich and poor, ordinary and weird, young and old, native and alien. The Ocean Highway (U.S. Rt. 13) was, and still is, one of the main north/south East Coast routes and was traveled by many with various missions and some with no mission at all.

There were six ferries in the fleet: four were steam-powered and the remaining two, including the *Accomack,* to which I was assigned, were diesel-powered. The *Accomack* was smaller and faster than the others, and I learned to love this old vessel as if it were my second home. It took her about ten minutes less time to cross the Bay, or about one hour and fifteen minutes. The big advantage to this was that more time was spent at the dock because all the vessels were on the same departure schedule. Being an eager fisherman, I used this extra time for angling around the many poles and bulkheads at each terminal. I caught enough fish to keep the

Captain and me supplied. Actually, Captain Jimmy Hume was an avid angler, but he did not fish while on duty. Fishing from his ferry in his gold braided uniform, preoccupied with sport, would not make the proper impression on the many passengers who boarded the ferry under his ultimate care and authority.

The ferry ran nearly all night, and that was my favorite time because usually the traffic was lighter, and this gave me some time to read or whittle duck decoys. We worked eight hours on and eight hours off, and often, after getting off my watch, I did not go to my bunk.

As an indication of the times, there was a higher percentage of blacks traveling during night hours, probably because they could not find accommodations during the fifties. There was a juke box in a lounge area on the passenger deck with a lot of space around, which made an ideal dance floor. It was almost as much fun as fishing to watch these late travelers dance their way across the Bay to the turned-up juke box, in rough or calm weather.

On one late-night trip, a neat, but tired and worried-looking older man approached the counter and ordered a cup of coffee. The initial rush was over, and realizing the man was lonely, I talked with him for a while. He was familiar with the ferry crossing and had traveled this route many times as a hardware salesman. While it seems fate had not been kind to him for most of his life, recent months had been tragic indeed. He had lost his wife to cancer, and a grandchild had been paralyzed in an accident. On top of, and probably related to these unfortunate setbacks, he had recently lost his job, and I guessed that his qualifications and his age dictated that his next work would be menial. Now he was on his way to move in with his daughter and son-in-law in North Carolina. It was apparent that he had some trepidation about this arrangement, so we discussed the pros and cons of his new life and all its possible pitfalls.

Comparing the options of my life with his was like the waxing and waning of the moon. Mine was in the formative stage with many paths as choices, and I could guide and nourish my future. But age and its consequences were slowly channeling him into a chute, leaving few choices in the time remaining. Perhaps neither of us knew how little that was.

Finally, after three cups of coffee, he took a napkin and carefully wiped from the counter a couple drops that had fallen from the spoon he used for stirring. Finished, and satisfied with this little chore tediously performed so that no one else would be troubled with it, he held out his hand for a warm farewell to a stranger. He walked away slowly, altering his gait to compensate for the steady roll of the ferry as it headed south across the mouth of the Bay. I never saw him again. I thought about this fellow human for a while and the bad deal he had been given in life. It caused me to wonder about what life had in store for me, as I cleaned up the counter and tallied up the sales. However, my thoughts soon turned to getting off duty the next morning, going fishing with my girlfriend and planning for the future.

Soon the ferry docked and the cars began to move out from the lower deck. But as frequently happened, an automobile was without its driver, and the deck hands were sent up to the passenger lounge level to find the missing person. I joined in the search expecting to find a tired passenger sound asleep in one of the comfortable chairs or laid out on a bench.

We looked everywhere, including the head, but no one was to be found. Then we came upon a neatly folded pair of pants and a shirt lying beside the juke box and almost hidden by a door that had been folded back. On these clothes was a pair of shoes and socks lined up as if they had been placed there by a gentleman's valet. Beside the shoes were a set of car keys and a thin and worn wallet. I nervously opened the wallet, and the Pennsylvania driver's license pictured my briefly-known friend.

As is often the case in the Chesapeake Bay, his body

was never found. I am sure that this weary man wanted it that way so as to trouble no one.

The second mate drove the car slowly off the ferry. I glanced into the window and saw a lifetime of possessions neatly arranged on the seats and on the floor of this old but well-maintained vehicle. In a paper bag on the back seat were several neatly wrapped Christmas presents.

Our ferry reloaded and turned back across the black, cold Chesapeake. Soon the sun would be up, and I would have two days off to fish, boat and hunt on this beautiful body of water—a playground for me and a tomb for my transient friend.

FIRST DEGREE

There were only two minor obstacles—grades and money.

It all ended in my hometown Post Office, and it all began about seven years before at Central High, when a tall pretty brunette caught my fancy. Actually there were plenty of other pretty girls here on the Eastern Shore of Virginia peninsula. The problem with them was they were either from the Bayside or the Seaside, and because we had been to school together for several years their novelty had worn off. But this girl was from New Jersey. Her origin, coupled with the fact that she was Roman Catholic, made her downright exotic.

When she told me she was going to college, I decided it would be strategic for me to go also, even though we would go to different institutions. This decision was made during my junior year of high school, and as you can see it was not a thirst for knowledge that led me to higher learning.

There were only two minor obstacles—grades and money. Fortunately, my high school principal, Leonard

167

Johnson, thought I had the ability to absorb some higher learning (I was far from saturated) and he altered my grades, placing me in the upper half of the class. I have always thought he did this because my mother was a Custis. He had married a Custis, and he seemed to respect this ancient Virginia name. For whatever reason, he was a good friend, and without his help I would not have been able to attend college.

One partial solution to the financial problem was solved when I met the two rigid qualifications for a scholarship: to be born and raised on Virginia's Eastern Shore and to be male. For the geographic requirements, I had, never been off the Shore until age fifteen, except for a few months that I spent with my parents when they lived and worked in Newport News during the war. And I could tell from endocrine feelings and interests that I was all male.

Of course, my mother and father helped me as much as they could. My father was a hardworking carpenter and cabinet maker. My mother worked days in a shirt factory and, after preparing supper for her family, ran the concession stand at the Idle Hour Theater in the evenings. And, when I was fourteen, I had started a small boat-building business, so this all helped. If I could keep the boat-building going, I might survive the four years until graduation. Then I could return home, work on the water, forget college and consider myself a success.

The first problem was getting me to Charlottesville. It was not felt that the family truck could climb the hills, which begin soon after you proceed west of Richmond.

However, two of my older outdoor companions, Cabell Mapp and Bill Mason, solved this. They, their wives and I piled into Cabell's Studebaker and we headed south on Route 13 to catch the ferry to the Western Shore and thence west.

I felt very comfortable in this car, because Cabell and I had used it for years to spotlight rabbits at night. In these models the front fenders were made so you could sit astride them and have the headlight between your legs and hold on as you went through brush, across fields and down bumpy dirt roads.

The trip to the University of Virginia was uneventful. My friends left me at the dormitory, returned to my homeland, and I was on my own.

The only time I had been so lonely was when I was lost on the Chesapeake Bay one foggy night. My Montgomery Ward outboard had quit and the fog rolled in "on little cats' feet" before I could reach shore. My only companions were tankers going to and from Baltimore, mournfully sounding their fog horns from every direction, but never becoming visible, which I suppose was good.

As I overcame the acute stage of loneliness, I began to learn my way around campus. Speaking a dialect reasonably similar to all these new people, I quickly became aware of my shortcomings, some of which were social, financial and academic.

Because of its renown as a party school, the University attracted rich boys from Virginia plantations as well as from up north. Many of these students had been to private schools or academies. Some had been educated by private instructors. The rest went to high schools, which, each year, graduated more students than had attended mine in its entire history.

There was one exception, however, and this was my roommate. Somehow, without a computer, the authorities had found another semi-literate country boy and put us in the same room so we would feel at home—as long as we never left it. He was a good fellow and is still a friend today. However, he could take it for a week only and went back to his family farm near Pungo, Virginia, not far from the North Carolina line, to be close to his girlfriend. The power of love can work in opposite ways.

In all colleges I suppose that you must do a lot of queuing up during orientation, or disorientation, according to how it affects you. There were lines for class registration, books and tuition. It was here that I first became aware of my humble qualifications and sensed that my fraudulent high school grades were going to become apparent and expose me as an imposter. While waiting in these lines, many students talked routinely of subjects far beyond my comprehension, and I learned that many took placement tests and skipped years of study, while I had to begin some subjects all over again.

Now that I was at college, theoretically I had to decide in which field to take my degree four years later. This seemed to be a far-fetched hypothetical question because I was certain to starve or flunk out before someone handed me a sheepskin.

I had originally wanted to be an architect, but that was a five-year course and my hard-won scholarship was for four years only. Prospects for a fifth year were dim, as I was already stretching my mental and financial limits to try for four.

My next choice was chemistry. I had been interested in this subject ever since dynamiting and poisoning fish in the Chesapeake Bay with Cabell Mapp.

However, one of the required subjects for a major in this course was German, and my high school language was Spanish. This meant I would have to start from scratch, since my complete repertoire in German was "sauerkraut." Thus, I signed up for German 101. However, it soon became apparent that it was beyond my ability to learn the peculiar letters and the strange way words and sentences were jumbled together. The savants felt it was necessary for chemists to be able to read the old German chronicles on this subject, but I deemed this unnecessary and "the" University now agrees with me. Now it is too late, and all I can do in this field is put salt on my scrambled eggs. In all fairness, however, I have mastered German numbers.

At this formative point in my education, I chose a path in the field of liberal arts, which was very flexible until the junior year, and I really did not think I would make it that far anyway. Besides, my educational inspiration had found another boyfriend who was handsomer, richer and smarter.

In my travels around the campus, and in the classroom, I would regularly encounter the same faces and same voices and would recognize and even get to know some of them. As the weeks went by I began to sense that some faces were not showing up. I was not sure who was missing or when—it was an insidious feeling of things happening that I did not understand, the same feeling I have when I feed my ducks and, without counting, gradually realize some of them have shown up missing. Gradually I realized that many of the students who had disappeared were those I had assumed were brilliant and would run the world and perhaps give me a menial job after I flunked out.

It was rare that I had enough money for an entire week of subsistence and usually hitchhiked home on Wednesday, Thursday or Friday to eat as much as possible, hoping to coast through the lean period ahead. Also, I was building boats in my father's carpenter shop, and this income was indispensable. The trip was a minimum of eight hours each way and required a ferry ride across the Chesapeake. This segment of the journey took about 1½ hours and usually required a wait for the next ferry. After my first year of college, I worked on these ferries and got to know many of the captains and crews. One of them, Captain Stanley

Parks, would delay leaving the dock if he saw me in the distance running to catch the ferry. Usually the person in charge of collecting the 95¢ toll would allow me to ride at no charge—a tremendous help to my budget.

I hitchhiked so often that many of the motorists recognized me with my thumb out and foot on my suitcase, which displayed a large "UVA" sticker. This sticker not only labeled me a nice guy, but occasionally it was recognized by alumni, who would offer me a lift and talk about the school and their own good times there.

Once, an old maid school teacher picked me up on a cold winter day, and after I had taken my seat beside her, we began to talk. She, too, was returning to the Eastern Shore for the weekend, as she always did, feeling the same yearning as I for the Bay, the ocean and home. She said to me, "I have watched you hitchhike for two years, so I figured you must be all right and decided to give you a ride." She gave me several rides after that, but in my Senior year I noticed that our paths were not crossing. I began to inquire and learned she had died.

Life in the dorms, even though females and cooking were prohibited, was largely ungoverned. There was no curfew, and one could drink or smoke at any time. Each room contained bunk beds and, because my roommate got there a few minutes before me that first day, I had to sleep on the top. When he departed, I moved down and took over the bottom bunk.

There were about twelve rooms on each hall, and we all got to know each other pretty well. There were boys there from all walks of life and I believe you could say I was from the slow walk. Some took an interest in my tales of the Eastern Shore, and I frequently would take one of them home with me for a weekend of fishing and country girls, or hunting and country girls—depending on the season.

One of my favorites was a friendly bully named Jim St. Clair from West Virginia. He was a football scholarship recipient and an excellent student—a rare combination. He loved to throw his weight around in a playful manner, and many of the students received his attention. One day he grabbed me, and in a second he was on his back on the concrete floor of the dorm. All the students enjoyed this spectacle. Thereafter, we would wrestle about two nights a week just to entertain the troops. I could always flip him onto his back during the first few seconds of the encounter, but after that his weight and brawn would tire me out, and eventually he would win. I think he always hoped I would not throw him, and I always hoped he would not tire me out, but neither of us achieved his goal.

The other entertainment was for me to consume a whole chicken while others watched and, for a while, this was a weekly event. This came about after one of the students observed me eating a chicken neck. I commented that when I got hungry I could eat an entire chicken—bones and all. The bet was on, and a collection was taken up to buy a whole fried chicken. If I ate it all, I would not have to pay

174

for it. Along about Wednesday or Thursday my weekly allotment would run out, so this was a windfall.

This went on for several weeks until some smart-alec from New York pulled an underhanded trick on me. Somehow he found a 20-year-old rooster, which he had prepared for the feast. Of course, the bones were hard and brittle, not at all like the usual young fried chicken. I could not swallow the bone splinters, so I lost the bet and the show never reopened.

Early on, I missed the country and decided to grow sweet potatoes in my room. My mother frequently put a potato in a bowl of water and allowed the vines to grow, bringing a little greenery to our home in winter. A goldfish bowl was a perfect vessel for this, and then goldfish were added. They seemed to like the profuse roots for hiding and certainly the roots benefited from their fertilizer. This made a perfect microcosm of symbiosis. My vines far exceeded anything my mother had grown, and the foliage from the two potatoes almost covered the ceiling.

In our sophomore year Jim and I decided to room together in the "old dorms." Now that we had completed the freshman year, we were free to choose our habitation. Usually we got along well, but when two people are in close continuous contact, sometimes tempers flare over trivialities. This happens to trappers in the north country, sailors at sea and, once in a while, to college roommates. We were not supposed to cook in our rooms, but we hid a hotplate in my trunk and heated canned soup and beans. Recently, Jim reminded me of my anger the time he spilled soup in my trunk.

Adjoining our bathroom was the residence of an upperclassman who inconsiderately dominated the facilities. This was a constant irritation to us as we tried to get to classes on time.

One day we found a dead crow and decided to make a present of it to our adjoining colleague. We carefully hid it in his room under some clothes in a chest of drawers. Soon he began to complain about a strange smell. The housing department sent plumbers, exterminators and various other professionals to determine the source of the foul odor, but all failed. Eventually the victim discovered the remains of the carcass, which had physically permeated the wooden drawer. Fortunately, he never found out who did this, but unfortunately he still took his time with his toilet.

My junior year found me continuing in a precarious financial situation but gaining confidence in the academic field. However, I still couldn't decide on a major, until the day I happened to see a sign on a professor's office door: "Anthropology." This was a newly offered course that interested me because it was the study of primitive societies. And it was right down my line because, ever since I had been a student in Charlottesville, I had felt I was the product of a primitive society; this line of study would make me feel

176

right at home.

This subject was taught by a young professor named Eric Wolf. He was a great teacher, and while anthropology didn't enable me to make big money upon graduation, it gave me a subtle understanding of life. It is an understanding I could not have gained from more lucrative fields of study, and it serves me to this day.

Times have changed at "the" University, which seems to be the trend everywhere. I will describe these changes to you without comment, and you will see that some were for the better and some were not.

In the early 1950s, there were no minorities and no women enrolled. The honor system was effective and everyone's word was taken as good. You could smoke or chew in class, but you had to wear a coat and a tie. It didn't matter if it was Harris tweed and silk from Eljo's or my threadbare Sears-Roebuck special.

In my college days, you were expelled in disgrace if a female was caught in your room, but now, I'm told boys and girls shower together. The honor system was very effective in days gone by at the University of Virginia, and one could leave a billfold on a library table or elsewhere on the grounds without fear of its ever being taken. I was visiting not long ago and went into the library, which had been my sanctuary while a student, and noticed that now one is electronically frisked on leaving the building. These days there is obviously no dress code, and most students are adorned in T-shirts and dungarees.

I merely mention these facts and emphasize that I

express no opinion on the correlation of any of them. They are simply the product of unstoppable trends permeating most of the world and are based upon the awakened spirit of man, which will lead us all somewhere. I'm not sure where.

Finally, there came the time for my graduation. Not being inclined to pomp and ceremony, I skipped this ritual and packed up my papers, goldfish, potatoes, books and wardrobe and headed home. Two weeks later, as I stood in my hip boots, my genuine sheepskin diploma was handed to me by Mr. Willis, our Postmaster in Belle Haven.

THE YEAR OF THE MICE

. . . I turned the boat in a circle and the mouse turned also, just like a compass needle.

It had been a bad year for mice. They were everywhere—almost like lemmings. The hardware stores were sold out of mouse traps, and each new shipment was bought up by a desperate public eager to rid itself of these pests. Thus, I suppose you would say that, from the perspective of the mousetrap business, it had been a good year.

The hawks, especially the kestrel, would probably consider it a good year for mice. I sat on my back porch and watched these falconettes perched strategically on the power lines that ran above a grassy field. From this vantage point, they look for mice and frequently plummet to earth, about three out of four times flying off with a tiny morsel of squirming rodent.

These predators did not return to the wires for dining but preferred to go to a tree after securing their meals. I would guess that a limb or bark was a more stable eating place than the wire.

From their head movements, one could easily see when something had attracted their attention. Their bodies would remain stationary, but the heads and necks moved side to side to offer a slightly different angle of view. Because they were about thirty feet in the air and the mice were seldom directly under them, it would seem that the angle of view would change so infinitesimally as to make no difference. Many birds show this same behavior, especially owls, and nature is so logical, so purposeful, so conservative, that I am certain there is a reason behind this. Gesticulating and wasted motion seem to be human traits.

Occasionally these predators would hesitate in their headlong attack, pull up and hover as their prospective meal disappeared from view. Sometimes they would quickly dive again. Otherwise they would return to their perch and wait for another opportunity.

The big redtails, in fewer numbers than the sparrow hawk, also came for the bounty. They did not perch on the wires, but preferred the top of utility poles or a substantial tree limb for their waiting place. At times they circled and plummeted to earth for a mouse. Their dive was much less steep than the sparrow hawk, and they were not nearly as successful. Ideally, they are better designed for larger prey, such as cottontails and gray squirrels. I know that the owls are very good at mousing from looking at their pellets, but I seldom got the chance to see them foraging.

On occasion I saw the red fox roaming the field for these tiny tidbits, which he devoured on the spot and then continued hunting, frequently jumping into the air for a better view of his scurrying prey.

So while some would say it had been a bad year for mice, many would say it had been a good year. It just depends on your mode of survival and your niche in the food chain. In nature and life, every feast has its famine, and every famine its feast.

There are two kinds of mice here in Eastern Virginia— the house mouse and the field mouse. The former is an introduced species, along with the ordinary (Norway) rat. They both came here as stowaways on ships centuries ago. Neither the house mouse nor the rat is very appealing in appearance or habit. But keep in mind that a rat of average IQ is smarter than a two-year-old human. Of course, we all know that smartness is not necessarily an admirable trait in someone other than yourself.

The field mouse is, on the other hand, a very attractive little animal. Its coat is a fawn color with white legs and pink feet. Due to its nocturnal habits, it has large protruding black eyes and large well-developed ears. But its habits are not much more appealing than those of its European cousin. As a result, both species are lumped together as undesirable vermin when they encroach upon humans. I doubt if many know that there is a difference—a mouse is a mouse.

The aversion that humans have to mice and rats is exceeded only by their distaste for snakes. However, just a few generations ago, one was considered fortunate indeed to have a black or king snake take up residence in a barn or especially a corn stack. Invariably, the grain attracted rats and mice and nothing, not even the domestic cat, is as efficient as a snake for keeping these rodents under control.

But alas, man's perception of his fortune does not include snakes in his houses or outbuildings, and instead of pitting nature's creatures against each other in a Darwinian way, we now resort to poisons and traps.

The mainland, of which the grassy field is a part, is not the only area where I noticed an increase in mice this past year. There is a three-mile strip of sandy beach bordering the Chesapeake on this same parcel of land. Between these dunes and the low pine woods about a mile away is a marsh composed of black needlegrass, salt meadow hay and ponds of brackish water.

On the widest and highest of these dunes, about midway from Nandua Creek to Craddock Creek, I have a one-room cabin. In this entire stretch of dunes there is not one mouse other than the field mouse. It seems that the European house mouse does live up to its name and prefers to cohabit with humans. Irrespective of this distribution of the two species, the field mouse had a great year on the beach.

The previous year I had made some alterations in the plumbing in this cabin, which left additional access to that already existing. This, coupled with the rodent population explosion, caused more than the usual mouse traffic through my wilderness retreat.

To cope with the problem, I purchased two dozen mouse traps. The type I obtained was truly a better mouse trap. These snapped open and set themselves when one end was pressed. A little peanut butter spread on the tripper mechanism made an irresistible bait. When a mouse met its demise (sometimes I caught two at a time), all one had to do was press the opposite end of the trap again; and the mouse would fall out and the trap was reset—a simple one-handed, actually two-fingered, operation. After using steel wool to plug all the holes and cracks in which a mouse could enter, I set up a trapline of about twenty of these better mouse traps around and close to all four walls of the inside of my cabin. A mouse uses its whiskers to feel its way around and therefore likes to stay close to walls. It loves confinement on at least one side if nothing better is available. There is a biological term for this, but I can't remember it now.

These traps had been set for about a week. The weather had been cold and windy, and the beach in front of my cottage is not a pleasant place to disembark and embark when the wind is very strong from offshore, as it had been lately. But now the sun was out and the wind had subsided, so I ventured out Craddock Creek into the Bay and north along the shore to my cabin to see if I had any luck; good luck for me that is, but bad luck for the little squatters that had been such a filthy nuisance.

As my skiff picked up speed and planed across the waters, the movement disturbed a stowaway. A field mouse came out from under the deck and began running fore and aft. It tried in vain several times to climb up the sides of my plastic boat, but fell back each time. Then, finding a foothold next to the area where a seat connects to the sides, it managed to reach the deck and immediately plunged overboard and swam for shore.

At first, I didn't notice its course since it had to swim one way or another and, although we were not in a lake, land was in every direction more or less, except for a small angle. Also, the nearest land was not a whole lot closer than the farthest land. However, immediately upon hitting the water, the mouse headed directly toward the shoreline from whence it came in a straight line and a very determined manner. The plight of this fellow creature had an immediate effect on me. Pathetically battling nature for its life in a confrontation forced upon it by man, the mouse reminded me of my own predicaments in the cold Chesapeake: sculling with one hand while bailing a leaky, wave-swept skiff with the other as I chased a crippled duck, or was lost in the fog, unable to see the bow of my boat. So I turned my boat around with the intention of scooping up the tiny rodent in a five-gallon plastic bucket, having nothing more suitable. My path took me between the mouse and its destination. I made a pass at him, but he was so quick in the water that I missed him. He turned away from the boat for a moment and, until I was clear of his path, he swam in the opposite direction. As I continued on past him to turn around for another try, he reversed his temporary direction and headed for the nearer shore again. I made another unsuccessful try to capture him, again putting my vessel between the water-soaked creature and the land from which we had departed and which he was struggling to regain. The same thing happened, exactly as on my first attempt to rescue him. However, on my third pass, he was so exhausted I was able to scoop him up along with several inches of water.

His prospects for survival had now increased. The water was still over his head and he could not see his destination, so I don't imagine he felt much better about things as he desperately tried to climb the white plastic walls of the bucket.

Paying close attention to his plight, I had turned the boat around to repatriate him when I noticed that he was swimming and struggling to climb on the opposite side of the bucket, which was now between him and his home shore. There was, of course, a good chance that this could be the result of coincidence. Being of a curious mind in these kinds of situations, I turned the boat in a circle and the mouse turned also, just like a compass needle. Regardless of which way I went, he still tried to swim in the direction of the closer shore. This was my mouse. He was my responsibility and I had grown attached to him, so I proceeded to the shore and released him on dry land. He ungratefully disappeared into the grass.[7]

I continued on my journey, which had begun with saving the life of a field mouse. My destination was the cabin trapline, where I was causing wholesale death to unwelcome squatters of the same species. Then, belatedly, I began to ponder (which is one of my characteristics): Was

---

[7] There will undoubtedly be some skeptical animal behaviorist out who may try to duplicate this experiment. If his results are not exactly the same as mine, then he just got hold of a dumb mouse. My mouse was smart.

the mouse orienting itself to the nearest land or its home turf? To answered this, all I needed to do was approach land on the opposite side, throw the mouse over and see which way he went. I will resume this experiment on a warmer day, with a bucket of mice, and record the result for science.

On the way to my cabin there was an all-terrain vehicle parked on a ramp along the north end of the beach. Here I was to encounter more mice. I stopped in order to start the motor so the battery would not run down in the long interval of non-use. When I raised the hood of the vehicle, the first thing I saw was a nest of some kind on top of the motor. I cautiously probed into it, not wishing to disturb its occupant, if any. However, this was not to be, for at first touch a mother field mouse dashed out. I knew for sure that it was a mother, because dangling from her breasts were six pink babies, all hanging on by their teeth.

Again, acting as a self-appointed god and either savior or executioner of mice, as my whims dictated, I closed the hood, replaced the canvas cover and continued on my way, their home undisturbed.

Suffice it to say, at my cabin I had ten dead mice in twelve traps. One had two. I did not try to revive any.

Whenever I catch two of anything at the same time, I

am reminded of my old friend, Mitt Bundick. If he and I caught two fish in a net, two squirrels in a trap, or two clams on a rake, regardless of the season he would insist that they were mating. I am sure that the first thing he would say if he had seen the two mice in one trap is, "Look, Bill, these two mice were mating." He never confirmed the sex of the accused, and I suppose he was so sure of his verdict that there was no need to check. One thing was certain: the mice were sure mating this year.

ARNIE

He had an odd assortment of attributes and handicaps
and would probably have been better off if he had all of one or the other.

Arnie read a lot. He probably read more than I, and that is a lot. And it is also embarrassing, when you consider the entirety of the thing. You see, there was something wrong with Arnie, or you may say something right, depending on your perspective. He was different is perhaps a better way of saying it. This difference relegated Arnie to a role that stipulated he would not succeed in life, either physically or mentally.

It was a tragic difference, but it was interesting and somewhat of an enigma. I still haven't figured it all out. If only his better points could have been combined with the few that I have, and vice versa, both of us might have gotten someplace.

When I first met Arnie, he was destitute, and I know that has not changed. He was small, neither black nor white, had a silly little round Elmer Fudd face, full of pock marks, acne and a big smile. He was more trouble than he was worth, but he needed help so he was given a job, or one may say adopted. We tried to train him to do various chores, and it was almost hopeless. But finally we thought he would do less harm cleaning than anything else, so he was put to work around our gallery sweeping, picking up trash, bringing wood to the fireplace and tasks of that nature.

He began to take a liking to me and showed me a respect I seldom received. I first noticed this when one day he closed my door before turning on the vacuum cleaner to clean the gallery space outside my office. He said, "Dr. Turner, I'm going to close your door because I'm sure you'll be doing some big deals on the phone and I don't want to disturb you." He was absolutely right, except the deals weren't all that big—I suppose they were big to Arnie—but his consideration and thoughtfulness were appreciated as well as flattering. Arnie closed the door, and I felt so important I thought I should smoke a cigar.

A few days later I encountered Arnie in the gallery. He stopped me and said, without hesitation, "Dr. Turner, you're a tycoon." Well, I liked the ring of that and proudly smiled. But he was not through—he then asked me if I knew how he knew that I was a tycoon. I replied in the negative, and he was pleased to be able to put me right. He gave me a very serious look, as if he were a professor explaining a difficult and important point to an apt pupil, and began: "Well, Dr. Turner, all tycoons is quiet and you is quiet and so you're a tycoon." Well, of course he was right, all the way around.

One day I decided to take Arnie on a journey to my farm six miles away. This was to be his longest journey to date. Until that time, he had never been more than five miles away from his birthplace. I showed him how to get into the car and put on his seat belt, and we were off. As we rode along, we discussed philosophy, the classics, history and other subjects, and we each learned something—a truly symbiotic conversation. We rode down the lane to my land and entered the yard. He seemed impressed, and we rode down to the waterfront. As we came to a halt, he looked with interest and said, "Dr. Turner, I see you have a gazebo." I looked around expecting to see an exotic animal bounding along the shore, but he pointed to my dock on Folly Creek. I suddenly realized what he was talking about. I had always wondered what I should call that imposing structure at the end of my pier where my boat was docked. When I got back to my office, I looked up this word, and sure enough he was right.

We ambled around my farm, and he explained to me the finer points of Victorian architecture, the rise and fall of the tides, the importance of marsh grass, how the greenhouse effect was the cause of my erosion problems and even the history of Folly Creek, beginning when it was a port of entry. Then I showed him my chickens, and he asked me how many were in the small flock. I told him I had six.

Arnie reminded me, although I have never seen one, of a Jaguar with a Model T Ford engine, or at times perhaps the reciprocal of this. He had an odd assortment of attributes and handicaps and probably would have been better off if he had all of one or the other.

Arnie was with me for several months until one day he didn't come in, but called to say that his brothers were taking him north to a big city (Hoboken, I think it was) where he would be better off. This concerned me. I figured I would be better off, but wasn't so sure about Arnie. I was reluctant to let him go.

However, one could not buck the lure of the North. There was nothing to do but outfit him for his adventure and wish him well. In turn, Arnie expressed his appreciation by giving me a bottle of fresh wine from the grocery store. *Boar's Head* was the brand, and it had been aged on the back of a truck. I valued this gift and, consequently, have consumed it in a conservative manner. However, when I feel down, I unscrew the cap and take a sip or put some over my ice cream. It tastes good either way, and it always reminds me of Arnie.

THE ULTIMATE BUREAUCRACY

Although this bureaucrat had obviously committed to memory the voluminous OSHA manual, he did not know anything about the Fourth Amendment.

I'm sure that you have heard this freely-used expression before, but in this case she really was a "cute little thing." I am referring to a lady (at least I assume so, with no evidence to the contrary) who appeared at the door of our business on an otherwise dreary, rainy September day in 1992. She said she represented the Occupational Safety and Health Administration on a state level and she wished to inspect me, by which she naturally meant my bronze casting operation. Under the circumstances, I was not adverse to her entering, despite the fact that only recently I had been inspected and fined for a few minor violations.

On this previous occasion, I was visited by a couple of triple dippers (i.e., they were retired army officers, getting social security and now employed by the bureaucracy). It seems to me that just one would have been a gracious plenty, but you know how it is in a bureaucracy, or perhaps it will suffice to say: "You will know if you have the patience to read this whole thing."

Anyway, these ex-generals had assured me that they had punished me for every trespass imaginable in the book and I was now clean, and let me say that the OSHA laws are very complex, very confusing and very many. In fact, one could take the OSHA bible of commandments and shut down any hospital, school or church in the United States without getting past the preamble.

So, I explained to this blue-eyed, blonde OSHA representative that I had already been inspected by her office and had paid my dues. She replied that her predecessors represented the accident division and she was in the disease division and had no interest in the former. Therefore, being certain that my institution, employing 25 citizens working diligently and honestly to support their families, harbored no disease, she was allowed to enter and look for evidence of the same.

I accompanied her on a tour of our facility, which manufactures "graven images." We went into every department and she carefully took numerous notes. I assumed that she was looking for germs that needed to be killed before an epidemic of some sort spread through my foundry and wiped us all out—you can't be too careful nowadays. After about an hour, she told me that she wished to speak with me in my office after she interviewed some of my employees.

While she was interviewing, I went to my office and set up a tape recorder. I did this because the entire inspection had been illegal, and I anticipated this could be verified by taping our conversation. You see, in Virginia, the law says that you do not have to allow an inspection from OSHA or any other law enforcement agency without your consent or a court order. The law goes on to say that consent must be obtained **and** identification must be presented. In this case, I had given consent, but she had not shown any identification, which would have been a plastic card with her photograph, age and measurements.

Everything went right from the very beginning. No sooner had she sat down than she pulled out a card, presented it to me, and said, "Here is my identification."

I replied in a very audible way for the hidden microphone, "I see that you are now presenting identification after gaining entry to my facility, and the law requires that you do this beforehand."

She began to get a little nervous and said I could do a "Miranda Act" or call her supervisor if I wished. I did not press the issue at this time because I always like a good legal scrap and I didn't want to get into an overkill situation in the very beginning. I did give her a little lecture about laws applying to enforcer as well as enforcee and let it go at that. We chatted on a little more about some bureaucratic nonsense—I've forgotten exactly what—and she concluded by saying she would be back in a month.

I eagerly looked forward to her next visit and on the appointed day combed my hair and had a crease put in my pants. On this occasion, she carefully identified herself and secured permission to enter, just as the law says. This just goes to show you how quickly women can learn if you spend a little time with them.

We then sat down to discuss the disease situation at my foundry. Although in most respects we had done well, she presented me with a citation concerning our compressed air outlets. These offending outlets each had a control valve lever on the end so that, according to how hard the lever was pressed, one could emit up to 100 pounds of pressure. The law, however, required that they be so regulated that 30 pounds was the maximum possible pressure. This law is the result of some factory workers in Hoboken, N.J., squirting air up a fellow employee's rectum, all in jest. I can see that air so administered could cause some bloating, but here in conservative Virginia we just did not indulge in that kind of behavior.

Along with the citation was a letter explaining that I was to pay a fine of $1,000. Included was a self-addressed envelope, but I had to furnish the stamp. Of course, I had no intention of paying this fine if it had been $1.00 with a self-addressed stamped envelope, and I telephoned the bureaucrat who had signed the form letter to let him know. I explained to him that I had read the Fourth Amendment and had decided to pay no more bureaucratic fines and asked him to make a notation in my dossier that henceforth a conviction by two consecutive judges (lower court and appeals court) would be required for me to consent to a fine. Although this bureaucrat had obviously committed to memory the voluminous OSHA manual, he did not know anything about the Fourth Amendment. He said that he was really a good guy to allow me to be fined only $1,000, and

that if I went to court the man "in the long black robes"
might even send me to prison. I told him right away that he
was wrong, because I knew the judge, who was once my
personal attorney and patient, and that he generally wore the
same old sports jacket. And he wasn't encouraged that I
knew this judge was of the highest caliber and would not be
prejudiced either for or against me. After refusing his
advice and ignoring his pleading to go along with the
system, we said goodbye. I followed up this conversation
with a confirming letter, a copy of the Fourth Amendment
and a jar of Elmer's glue so that he could paste it in his big
OSHA rule book.

It was not long after this that I received a summons to
appear in court.

For one who desires to keep his finger on the pulse of
the community, there are several places I recommend.
First, there is the barber shop. Men gossip much more than
women, and it is more spicy, more vindictive and just as
accurate. I have my hair done by a beautician on
appointment because of the demands of time, but I miss
hearing the men talk. Another prime location is the country
store, but such establishments are now almost gone and
those that are left are so disfiguratively evolved that they no
longer can be considered. The real place to feel the life
throbs of the community is in the lower court. With this in
mind, I went to the courtroom a little early on the day of
reckoning, hoping to get an idea for a story or two.

I took a seat beside two old ladies who seemed to
recognize me. Perhaps we had met at a party of some sort,

certainly not at a local benefit ball. The one with the most teeth, it turned out, had been convicted of poisoning her husband some years ago and was now out on parole. Of course she didn't do it, even though she honestly admitted to me that he deserved it. To her credit and despite this injustice, she didn't hold a grudge against the system, because she made a lot of new friends while serving her sentence. One of them was her companion, whom she had accompanied to court. Her cohort was accused of bootlegging but, of course, was also innocent.

I chatted with these two newly found friends while other cases were being heard. These conflicts were an ample reflection of the cross section of our rural society. One waterman wanted a divorce because his wife couldn't iron properly, but the judge turned him down. One elderly man had shot his neighbor's dog with mustard seed when it chased his tomcat up a tree. One young lady with her hair in curlers and chewing bubble gum insisted that the state trooper had pulled her over to flirt, then became aggravated with her when she resisted. They had different versions of what was being resisted. And so it went for an hour or so.

Just before my case was to be heard, one of my new friends offered me a dip of snuff and went on to tell me about her stay in a Swedish finishing school, daintily wiping a trickle of tobacco juice from one of her chins. I am not sure, but I don't think she graduated. I was getting a double dose of wonderful entertainment listening to these ladies and the witnesses on the stand.

Finally, however, my time came, and the assistant

197

district attorney and I approached the bench. I was charged with failure to have air hoses properly regulated, and my citation plainly stated that this was a violation of safety rules that was "likely" (an important word) to cause a serious or fatal injury.

I immediately asked the judge for a continuance so that I could have time to properly prepare my defense with discovery proceedings. The young attorney, a pleasant enough fellow, immediately insisted that this was a criminal offense and there could be no discovery.

From previous conversations with him I knew that he held this belief. However, my son, Bob, who is an attorney, had given me a copy of the statute, which explains that my violation was a civil offense and "all means of discovery are available." For theatrics, and to keep the opposition off guard, I had folded up a copy of the law that controlled my fate into a greasy little wad. It was with great humility that I slowly unwadded this paper, carefully cleaned it off with spit and respectfully asked the judge if I could please take the opportunity to explain the law to him and the young attorney, with whom he was in agreement so far. They both read the document with interest and could not disagree that I was entitled to discovery—just another word for harassment, dumb immaterial questions, fee building and delay. And in the legal profession, there is more money in delay than any of the other golden opportunities that lawyers have created for themselves by making laws that allow them to efficiently make money by being inefficient. Of course, in this case, it didn't apply to the young attorney, who was being paid on a salary basis and just wanted to dispense with me as quickly as possible and move on to the next potential criminal. I understood his position entirely, and I harbor no grudge.

After establishing my right to defend myself with discovery proceedings, it naturally followed that I must be given time to do so, and the judge allowed me a continuance.

Having won round one, I folded up the paper, replaced it in my pocket, said goodbye to the judge and the humbled young attorney. On the way out, I paid my respects to the two old ladies, one of whom was picking her nose, while the other daintily wiped away some more tobacco juice from another of her chins.

I did not look back as I left the courtroom, but I could see from the corner of my eye that the prosecutor had gathered his papers and was preparing to depart. There is nothing else to do after a judge has made a ruling. That is the end of it, and I knew this because I had seen it all on TV.

The next day my secretary told me I had a visitor, and one of my brand new old friends from my court appearance on the previous day was shown to my office. I again declined her offer of snuff. She quickly grabbed her lower lip, gave it a tug to create a storage space and dumped in a dab or so of her addiction while settling back into a chair across from my desk.

She got right to the point: "Dr. Turner, that's a kangaroo court where you was yesterday."

I asked why she had such a low opinion of a legal system that had only given her ten years for poisoning her husband. Then she explained, "No sooner had you left when that lawyer went back up to the judge and started talking about your case behind your back."

Well, this was an interesting turn of events. Right away I remembered another thing I had seen on TV, and I realized that my human, civil, legal, moral, constitutional and God-given rights were being tampered with. I was aghast. I telephoned my good friend, the Commonwealth Attorney, to complain of this dastardly deed of his cohort and made arrangements to see the former that same day. I put on an atmosphere of persecution and humbleness that would have drawn sympathy from the hardest of men.

When, on the verge of tears, I explained to the prosecutor what had happened (and reminded him that I was partially responsible for his being in this lofty position, which is another whole story), he immediately called the judge to ask for an audience. This was granted, so we crossed the street and went to his chambers. His Honor was sitting back with his feet on his desk next to a bronze sculpture I had given him. After I expressed my genuine concern, he assured me he was not prejudiced either way by the young attorney's comments to him after I had left the courtroom. (I knew this already, because this judge rightfully has an impeccable reputation.) I then assumed my "trusting-in-the-system" attitude and, because I considered myself the winner of round two, went back to my office and thanked the Lord for looking out for me so well, even

200

though I probably didn't deserve it.

I sat right down and wrote myself an indignant letter to every official in the state remotely connected with this audacious and foul attempt to deprive a defenseless citizen of his rights and denounced the bureaucratic and legal conspiracy behind the whole thing. I was on a roll and having a great time living on this edge.

The real fun, however, began when I issued my first request for documents and presented my first interrogatories to OSHA. Most will know what I mean, but I want to explain in case my snuff-dipping friend reads this—I think she was concerned about my future, and I want her to know that I was in control all along.

The citation said I was guilty of ten violations of a safety (not disease or health) rule that "were likely to result in serious injury or death." It was plain to me that if this were so, it would have been humanitarian of "Big Brother" to inform me of this danger immediately. The Freedom of Information Act allowed me to obtain copies of all notes, reports, etc., and I did this. My suspicions were confirmed when I saw that on the first visit the OSHA officer had noted the infractions in her report and was content to allow us all to be killed.

The word "likely" in the citation was a veritable feast of gray uncertainty. If one doesn't stop to think, it comes forth as a good solid definite legal word. However, as a citizen and defendant, I wanted to elucidate this meaning completely. After all, if it turned out that what I did or didn't do was "not likely" or "unlikely" to cause death or injury, I would be innocent and not go down on the record books of Accomack County as a violator of the law—a matter of importance to me. Therefore, to the consternation of the Volvo-driving yuppie lawyers working for the state, I decided to seek a definition of this word in my interrogatories.

To them, "likely" meant "likely" and nothing more; however, this was not to be. There is more than one factor that determines likely. Let me give an example: if you stand in your potato field during a thunderstorm, you are not likely to be killed by lightning. However, if you do this more than once you are, on the whole, more likely to be struck. If you expose yourself enough times, at some point you will cross the line where you pass from the unlikely to the likely. To be more precise, consider rolling the dice. The chances are that you are not likely to roll "snake eyes" the first time. But if you keep on rolling 36 times (6 x 6), you are likely to roll them. If you roll them 17 times, you are not likely (or have less than 50% chance), and if you roll them 19 times, then you are likely (or have more than a 50% chance) to roll snake eyes or any other combination of numbers.

As the reader may now be bored and irritated at having to read this, so were the lawyers for the state and the local assistant Common-wealth Attorney and his helpers from the state OSHA team. But they could neither define the word "likely" nor produce statistics that would uphold it after I defined it for them.

The word "serious" was equally ambiguous, but there was no question about "fatal." Like "square" or "pregnant," "fatal" has no gradiations.

My interrogatories covered many relevant questions, including the educational experience of the enforcer and technical items, such as air pressure, anatomy, statistics, etc. However, the question that gave them the most trouble was: "Why did you hide from me for a month the fact that a condition existed in my facility that was constantly threatening twenty-some employees with serious injury or death?" My question was never answered.

When it came to production of documents, they were downright stubborn. When they refused to meet my demands, I obtained a "ducus tecum," i.e., a court order requiring that they show me the requested documents in the local court house. Since we are in an isolated part of Virginia, this upset everybody except me.

Along about the third or fourth set of interrogatories and the third request for documents, and right after I gave them my witness list, which looked like a "who's who" roster of state officials, I received a phone call from the local Assistant Commonwealth Attorney. He said he had good news for me and my fine was going to be reduced to one half the original amount, or only $500. I told him I would think on it, but I got so involved with preparing the fifth set of interrogatories that I forgot to let him know my decision. About three weeks later he called me again and said my fine had been reduced to only $100. I explained to him that if I paid the fine, the press, which had planned to attend, as well as the two old ladies I had met in the courtroom, would be disappointed. In other words, it would be a classic anticlimax and just not fair to the public. He didn't seem real happy when he hung up.

About two weeks later, a couple of days after I let the state lawyers have their fourth "ducus tecum," the phone rang, and my secretary told me that the attorney wanted to speak with me. I knew exactly what he wanted before I picked up the telephone—the state was throwing in the towel. This was disappointing, and I begged him to not do that to me. I even offered to give the state $100 to prosecute me. So now I had gotten into that overkill situation, and there was no turning back.

It reminded me of a story I had read when I was child. You see, this good cowboy got caught by some bad Indians, and they were having a great time torturing him. Whenever he appeared to be about done-in, they fed and nursed him back to life so they could torture him again. But one day he fooled them and just up and died in the midst of a really good torturing session and spoiled all the fun.

THE PRODIGAL FIELD HAND

We pulled some brush over the grave to hide our miscalculation,
but the next day our grandfather saw it and told us to re-bury the goat.

Over the years, Elmer Leroy and I often wondered what happened to him. We didn't hire private detectives or advertise for a missing person, of course. But we mused about Jim Buggs and some other childhood acquaintances every couple of years or so on sunny days when the fish weren't biting. And there is nothing that promotes thinking about the past as well as a poor fishing day, when the water is calm, the sun keeps your brain from planning your future, and you are left with nothing but memories. As you grow older and your friends thoughtlessly pass on, leaving you in a minority, there is a tendency to prog around in the past and search for replacements. Lately, it seemed we had been losing old acquaintances faster than we could locate new ones.

Then suddenly, one Saturday night we were sitting around the club, which is really the Texaco station, drinking beer, scratching, watching the fights on TV, talking football during the ads and listening to the scanner, when our casual quandary about Jim resurfaced.

It had been a good evening on the scanner—we had got in on a woods fire, a lost hound, a husband beating and a holdup at a competitor's gas station—when we heard a deputy call in a Pennsylvania license plate number. He then told the people back at the control center in Accomac, the County seat, that he was following a big, shiny, new Cadillac with a chrome-encased spare tire on the rear, just like a migrant crew leader's car. He was as excited as a good rabbit hound on a hot trail as he described the aberrant behavior of his prey. It seems that this vehicle was driving on the right side of the road, within the speed limit, with no weaving in and out or any of those things that good, honest folks around here do. It was obvious to this young deputy that the driver of the car was desperately trying to be unobvious—a dead giveaway to anyone who has studied Criminology 101.

With the evidence mounting, the deputy decided to pull over this fancy car from up north and check it out. It was thrilling to sit there in the comfort of our rocking chairs and listen to the siren blast out a command of the people while we tried to piece together the unfolding drama.

The car was stopped not far from Shield's Bridge, and we waited incommunicado while the culprit was questioned. We could only imagine what was going on. After a beer and one round of the fight, in which a black guy was beating up on a poor white boy who stood no chance whatsoever, the deputy came back on the air to ask for a check of the criminal record of the car's driver, who claimed to be the owner—Jim Buggs—who had now been brought to bay.

It didn't hit me right away, but Elm pushed up instantly and put his ear up to the speaker. He was always quicker than I and would often have two birds down on a covey rise before I could raise my gun to my shoulder. Elm listened awhile for more information, then said to me, "Didn't Jim Buggs go up to Philly?" I agreed that I had heard a rumor to that effect one time, but I pointed out that the Jim Buggs we knew wouldn't be driving a Cadillac unless he was a chauffeur or a car thief.

The deputy came on the scanner again: "I can't find a thing wrong here—he even has a title to the car, and it's brand new—I figured at least he would be making payments on it."

The gum-chewing female voice at the control center said she couldn't find any criminal record on Buggs, who claimed he had come down to the Shore to see his mother, whom he had just taken home from church choir practice. Now he was on the way to see his sick sister.

Finally, the deputy replied, "I guess we're going to have to let this boy go; 10-4, over and out."

We cut off the scanner. Now the poor white boy was on the canvas, the referee was counting, and we had no hope whatsoever. We soon shut off the TV and went home.

One of Elm's friends knew the gum-chewing girl at the sheriff's station and got the address of Buggs up in Philly. Of course, this was against the rules, but it is surprising what a little pillow talk will do. Next, we got his phone number and called up there, and an English accented man answered the phone. Right away we figured we had dialed the wrong number. We were getting ready to hang up because of that accent and the smell in the phone booth, but we had paid for three minutes and wanted to use up our time some way. We left our names with the Englishman, who said Mr. Buggs was out of the country but would contact us when he returned. So we gave him the Texaco station number, knowing full well that this wasn't our old friend Jim Buggs, but we had never talked with anyone before who had been all the way out of our country and thought we might learn something. Besides, we thought if we got a long-distance call at the club, it would impress our friends.

This did get us to thinking about our childhood and the real Jim Buggs who was one of our best childhood friends. Elm, who was my cousin—although I didn't brag about it much—and I worked on our grandfather's farm every summer; he had about fifty acres on Craddock Creek next to the Bay. His farm had the usual tenant shacks, which were supplied free to the farm help. In exchange for this, the occupants were expected to have lots of children who were supposed to pull weeds, feed the livestock, hoe the corn and perform various menial chores. There were two families on our grandparents' subsistence farm with about ten offspring between them, although we never figured out which ones belonged to which parents. However, Jim and Jester, the two closest to our age, were not related. Jim was a tall, lanky, friendly boy about two years older than Elm and me. Jester was short, and although socially acceptable, not nearly as much fun as his colleague, Jim. What I did admire about Jester was an ornament that he wore on his foot—a penny with a hole in it and string running through the hole, fastened just above his left ankle.

All of the children worked and played together on the farm. The segregation, which I did not understand, was at dinner, served around noon after a hard morning's work. My cousins and I would sit at the table in the kitchen, and Jim and Jester would take their meal in the adjoining screened porch. Elm and I would vie for the privilege of taking fried chicken, potatoes and beans to our companions, who ate it as fast as we could go back and forth. Possibly, their evening and morning meals at home were less hearty.

Jim was not a world-class field hand. He would rather play than work and seemed to just coast along in the fields, getting by with as little effort as possible, waiting for the end-of-day swim in the creek. He always seemed to be dissatisfied with his lot and was happier in school. But his schoolhouse was about 25 miles away (a 2-hour bus ride daily), and this time on the road detracted from his required farm work. He reluctantly terminated his formal education when he was about twelve.

His dissatisfaction with farm life came to an abrupt ending in the summer of '45, although I think he had thought about it many times before while he was leaning on his hoe daydreaming. One day he, Elm and I were told to glean the fields for corn nubbins. Actually, Jim seemed to like this job, and Elm and I certainly did, because it was a chance to hook the family goat, Billy Joe, to a small cart and go for a ride. We had loaded up with corn, and Jim, being a little older, was at the helm. Billy Joe was a huge old animal with long, spiral horns and a spiraling odor equally noticeable. He was always stubborn on leaving the barnyard but would return home in a hurry. After we filled the cart with the runted and broken ears of corn that milestone day, Jim let him have his rein, and we held on tightly as we bumped across the field headed for the barn. All of us, including Billy Joe, were in good spirits as we entered the barnyard, when suddenly life changed for the goat and Jim.

As we charged into the barnyard, the left wheel of the two-wheel cart hit a pine stump, and we capsized. The three of us received a few additional scratches, but Billy Joe, strapped between the shafts, was flipped over on his head, and one of his horns broke off close to its base. It was a bad wound from which the blood flowed freely until my grandfather cauterized it with a poker from his blacksmith shop. In three days, Billy Joe died, and Jester, Jim, Elm and I were told to dig a grave to bury him.

A rope was put around his mangled head and hooked to one of the draft horses, and this sad entourage headed for the woods back of the cow pasture. After an hour of digging through roots, we thought we had the hole deep enough and rolled the heavy, bloated carcass in and covered it up. It was very hot work; we were sweating, tired and desperately wanted to wash our hands of this smelly affair as quickly as possible. But when we were almost finished filling in the grave, we detected that Billy Joe's four feet were still above ground. It seems our depth-perception was off. We pulled some brush over the grave to hide our miscalculation, but the next day our grandfather saw it and told us to re-bury the goat.

Billy Joe's living odor was not good, but when combined with the additional odor of decay it created a miasma of stench that we could almost feel. Besides, burying something is not so bad, but exhuming and re-burying a friend didn't appeal to any of us. Jester thought about it and said he had a solution. He went home and got his father's firewood saw, and we sawed off the legs and threw them in the creek on an ebb tide.

From then on Jim seemed more remorseful than usual, then he just disappeared, and not even his family knew where he was. Not long after that, Jim's parents' tenant house burned, and our grandfather had a bad year on the farm, so the Buggs family moved on. Someone heard a rumor that Jim went to Philly, but we had to keep on with life, and soon these memories, good and bad, faded.

We were sitting in the Texaco station one afternoon about two weeks after we heard about the yellow Cadillac when the phone rang. I had won the toss to do the talking if this Mr. Buggs were to call us as the Englishman said he would. I didn't know what I expected to hear, but I didn't expect to hear a long-distance voice say, "Billy, this is Jim—are you and Elmer Leroy still pulling weeds?"

Right away I knew it was our long-lost friend, and I put two and two together—got five—and asked him what kind of work he did for that Englishman. He just chuckled. Jim didn't have time for a long conversation right then, but said he was coming down to the "Shore" soon and wanted to see Elm and me. I offered to meet him at the bus station, and he was as appreciative as he was fifty years ago when I would hand him a nice chicken foot and a biscuit on my grandfather's porch. But he said that wasn't necessary and he would see us soon. In retrospect, I think he sensed we weren't going anywhere.

On his next visit down here, Jim stopped by the service station to see us. The first thing he did was have his gas tank filled up with premium high test! Our friends only got, at the most, five gallons of regular, so we hoped this impressed Alfred Joe, the owner of the gas station, who let us hang out there. We cleaned Jim's windshield so we could nonchalantly see his Cadillac close up. Then we all sat down on some soda pop crates and exchanged our missing half centuries. Ours wasn't too interesting so I'll skip that, but if you believed him, Jim's story was. Of course, we didn't—he was always a dreamer standing there in the cornfield propped up on his hoe with a rusty blade.

Jim said that he had never liked farm work, and after the goat episode, for which he blamed himself, he decided to go away and seek his fortune. He couldn't go south because he didn't have the fifty cents for the ferry ride across the Bay from Cape Charles to Norfolk. The only other way to go was north, and he caught a ride on a freight train when it stopped at Belle Haven siding to hook up with some potato cars. He climbed into one of these cars, but he was so weary of toting potato sacks on the farm that he couldn't sleep. The next morning he was in a city, which turned out to be Philadelphia, and he decided to disembark.

First he took a job at the freight terminal, which lasted for a few months. Then he obtained a position on a garbage truck emptying cans into the back of the truck driven by a white guy. Remembering the days when he was hungry on

213

the farm, he marveled at the waste of food as he performed his work. He thought if there were some way he could get all that food-type garbage down to Virginia to slop the hogs he would be a rich man. This first idea, although it was a good one, didn't work out because he couldn't get anyone to finance it. So he continued working as a garbage can dumper for a couple of years until he was promoted to driver. All the time he was saving money to attend school at night for his high school diploma.

He got to know a lot of people on his garbage route through South Philly and loved the cobblestones and concrete, free of dust and mud. However, he reasoned that, although he was earning a living hauling away spoiled food from the city streets, this was not too different from digging, picking and hauling it fresh on the farm.

Then one day the tide turned when an old widow lady's rusted-out garbage can fell apart while being emptied, and Jim kindly reminded her she would need a replacement if she were to continue receiving service. Feeling sorry for the old woman, Jim agreed to bring her a new can if she would reimburse him. Many people on his route had the same rusty-garbage-can problem, and if you have ever worked as a dumper on a garbage truck, you will know how it feels when you lift a full can and the bottom falls out, and you have to get down on your hands and knees and pick it up.

As a result of these incidents, Jim decided to keep a stack of new containers beside him in his truck. He sold these for a modest profit, purchasing them retail. The demand increased, and Jim located a surplus store, purchased the cans wholesale and (so he claimed) began to make big money. Jim then began to franchise out this idea to his fellow drivers, and he kept them all supplied with new cans and made money on practically every new garbage can in South Philly. He was employed by the city, and this practice was not exactly proper, but the officials turned a blind eye to his operation because it made the streets look better, the pick up more efficient and the citizens happy.

Jim next decided to go directly to the manufacturer of the garbage cans and save even more money on his cost. This worked out fine, and the money was really coming in a lot faster than it did digging potatoes and picking tomatoes on the farm. The really big money, if you were to believe Jim Buggs, began to come when he simultaneously expanded his operation into North Philly and Camden, New Jersey. Of course, he claimed at this time to not drive a garbage truck but instead have an office and staff of several white folks working for him. This last part was almost believable because Jim always treated Elm and me as equals, even though he was older and taller and shared anything he had, which wasn't much.

He told us everything is relative, and what he thought was big money then got to be small change later. This metamorphosis took place, so Jim claimed, when he designed a non-banging, raccoon-proof garbage can and had some people in Taiwan make them and ship them to Philadelphia.

All of these things, Jim said, really just gave him

spending change, which he invested in real estate. His wife was from Arkansas and wanted to retire there some day, so he bought a few acres that later turned out to be right in the middle of a new highway. Being modest and not wanting to give himself much credit, Jim said this was just luck. But this real estate deal just whetted his appetite and he parlayed his money (so he claimed), and eventually bought up half the county where his wife was raised.

This went on and on, and Elm and I were in a quandary. We would look at each other, the big yellow Cadillac, then at Jim.

Finally, Jim had to leave, but assured us he would come back and take us for a ride some day; we figured we had already been taken for a ride.

About a month later, Jim called and told us to meet him at the airport in two hours. Of course, we do have a nice 7,000-foot concrete runway close by. But I don't want to mislead you about this, so I will admit it was not the local economy that gave us this. Actually, it is a leftover from a World War II bomber training facility, and it is a great place to hunt rabbits at night. Now it is primarily used by rich sportsmen, businessmen and recreational pilots.

We arrived at the airport at the appointed hour and looked for the yellow Cadillac. It was not there, which did not surprise us. Many times Jim wouldn't show up in the fields until a half hour or more after sunrise, and we just figured he had not changed. We walked around the tarmac, waiting for Jim, and kicked on the airplane tires. On the verge of leaving, we heard the distant drone of an airplane and thought we might as well watch it land before we left.

A twin-engine plane became visible up in the north, flashed by the airport, made a graceful turn and landed into the north wind. It taxied up to the terminal (which at one time right after the war was a house of prostitution), spun around sharply and stopped. Elm and I then decided we would leave before one of these Yankee sports got out and started asking us a bunch of questions about the fishing. We turned our backs and were walking toward our pickup when we heard a familiar voice, "Elmer, Billy, where're you going? Let's go for a ride." We looked back, and our own Jim Buggs was descending the fold-out steps of this beautiful airplane as an impressive blonde-haired man in a pilot's uniform held the door. We remembered the last time we went riding with Jim and only agreed to get on the plane after we determined that he wouldn't be doing the driving.

All of this really didn't sink in until Elm and I were sitting back in soft, upholstered chairs drinking whiskey from a glass (Jim doesn't drink), cruising along over the Chesapeake at 300 mph while Jim actually gave orders to the captain of the plane. He told the young man in a polite but authoritative manner to circle over Craddock Neck so we could look down on our childhood playground. From the air we could easily see the remnants of the old saw dust pile, the foundation of Jim's long gone home and the approximate location of Billie Joe's grave. The eroded shoreline was dotted with double wides and tin trailers. An ugly asphalt road split the homestead right down the middle, and the swimming hole was silted in. Much had changed.

I well remember the pilot's reply, "Yes sir, Mr. Buggs, but don't forget you have to be in Hot Springs this evening for dinner with Mrs. Buggs."

Jim was always late; that's why we always knew he would never amount to much.

AUNT OPHELIA
AND THE POTATO BUGS

*Luke and Ophelia purchased a used cookstove and a crippled pig
and moved into a one-room shack on a worn-out farm
owned by an inbred white named George Trader.*

Ophelia was her name. Aunt was her title. She was
called Aunt Ophelia. Because she was black, you may think
that Aunt Ophelia was a patronizing appellation. It is true
that some who had the good fortune to be able to address
her may have thought of it in that sense; however, to those
who mattered, it was a title of respect—earned, not just
bestowed.

She was elderly, very fat, with a beautifully flattened
nose, big lips and an ample bosom. She sweated profusely,
possibly because of the chore of moving her bulk. I first
met her in our local hospital, a very dangerous place indeed,
unless serious life-threatening consequences forced upon one
have somehow statistically overshadowed the inherent
dangers of this institute of healing itself.

Now she was a sitter for my elderly friend and mentor,

Robert H. Rockwell, nearing the end of his productive life and wanting to do so in dignified comfort. When I walked into Room 221 that evening, the first thing that Aunt Ophelia told me was that Mr. Rockwell, who was in obvious pain, needed an enema. Of course, I didn't pay much attention because I realized instantly that she was not a real doctor, not even a registered nurse. However, it was readily apparent that Mr. Rockwell needed something.

I had not been there long when an intern condescended to pass through the portals (and collect $50). The first words he heard, or perhaps I should say the first directed at him, were from Aunt Ophelia: "Doctor, Mr. Rockwell sho do need an enema."

The brilliant young graduate of Harvard paid her no mind but began to address my well-traveled and well-read mentor in a childlike manner and made a cursory glance at his chart on the foot of the bed. After uttering a few brilliant words, he and his entourage went on to Room 222, where I suspect a healing of similar quality was administered.

After reminiscing with my dying friend, I left with the same reservations with which I have become accustomed whenever I leave anyone I value in this particular institution.

A couple of evenings later, I again visited Mr. Rockwell and once more found him in pain. Aunt Ophelia plaintively greeted me: "Yes Suh, he sho do need an enema." Soon the sophisticated young doctor returned to the scene. The same sequence of events occurred with the same patronizing attitude to the sitter and the sittee, except on this occasion Mr. Rockwell was given a shot to put him to sleep and prevent his wasting valuable medical time that could be used in visiting other patients at $50 per session. He dozed off, and I was alone with the sitter.

I had heard a few things about Aunt Ophelia's medical career since my first visit two days earlier. It is amazing how one can be exposed to a fact or a person for the first time, then in a short period obtain more and more information on this same new subject. So it was with Aunt Ophelia, and I had been told that she was once a midwife and how she had been widowed at an early age.

Thus, as Mr. Rockwell slept his remaining life away (the least troublesome way the doctor could find to ease his pain), I began to know his sitter. In a gentle voice she told me of her midwifing days, before she was forced out of business by the real doctors. It seems that her midwifing was mostly a service to the poor, which included some of the whites and all of the blacks. She would deliver several babies a week and made her rounds in a cart drawn by a mule. Usually she was not paid in cash but given a few hams, chickens or potatoes. Frequently the only pay she received was the honor of having the child named after her, and there are a lot of Ophelias roaming around the Bayside farms of lower Accomack County, her principal territory. She never mentioned her infant mortality rate, but I later learned that it was approximately half the rate of most real doctors.

This sequence of events occurred in Room 221 on at

least two more occasions, and Mr. Rockwell continued in pain with no attempt at a diagnosis and nothing done for him except placation and a shot of a barbiturate to make him sleep so he couldn't complain. Aunt Ophelia still insisted that he needed an enema, and finally the young doctor wrote this directive in the chart in a manner that would lead you to believe it was his own idea. On my next visit I could tell from the expression of Aunt Ophelia's face as I entered the room, that her patient was better. Indeed he was, and he spent an hour or so telling me about his collecting giraffes and lions in Africa in the early 1900s. However, his end was near, and he continued to become more feeble, certainly none the better for his belated attention. Not long afterwards, he died, in relative peace thanks to his observant sitter. At last he was free from the patronization that is so often directed at the old regardless of their intelligence or experience.

Aunt Ophelia remained in my thoughts over the years, and I began to pick up additional bits and pieces about her life, all of it interesting, especially the events which occasioned her widowhood.

About the same time Mr. Rockwell was collecting museum specimens in Africa, Ophelia was a teenage bride of a somewhat difficult, rebel-type field hand named Luke Satchell. He had earned this rebellious reputation because he was about seventy-five years ahead of his time in racial philosophy. Or perhaps he was just so foolhardy that he allowed his feelings of injustice, whether valid or not, to be known.

This couple had begun their short life together in a tar-paper shack in Hack's Neck. In those days this area was noted for its inbred whites (not in the aristocratic Egyptian sense). There was some geographical rationalization for all this. You see, this area is relatively low, and the land is not the best for farming or building. The poor whites and the blacks were economically forced into these rural ghettos, and everyone was somebody's relative. These poor did not travel much in those days; their poverty corralled them into this isolated area, and their horizons were seldom crossed.

I can remember when dating in high school that if someone took out a girl from Hack's Neck, he was looked upon with scorn for the foreseeable future, and the girls from the highland would be reluctant to accept an invitation. Most students from this area dropped out of school at an early age and never participated in athletic events.

Now just the opposite is true, and the place to be seen at a party is Hack's Neck. Many wealthy retired doctors, lawyers and exotic come-heres dwell on the waterfront in this fashionable area, and the plastic yacht has largely replaced the wooden work boat.

Luke's beginnings were obscure. He was not a native of this area. Nathan, Ophelia's father, found the boy alongside the railroad tracks when he was about five years old. There was no exact way of fixing Luke's birth date. It was pretty certain that he had arrived on a southbound freight, because no one had recalled seeing him the previous day, and the train came once a day in alternate directions. Furthermore, he wore an old coat that contained the label of

223

a Philadelphia clothier, so it was surmised that it had been salvaged from a garbage dump in that area. Apart from that, no one did much worrying about the origin of this small black boy—indeed, no one cared. It was just information that presented itself along with the boy.

Nathan was a farmer and field hand, the usual occupation of blacks in this area and era. Ballplayers, engineers and singers were a rarity in those days. He had been to the auction block with a crate of strawberries that day and had taken his place in the back of the line several times, only to be bumped by the white farmers whenever his turn to sell his produce was imminent. In frustration, he decided to just park his old mule and the cart in the shade and wait until some of his white brethren were finished before giving it another try. Being an industrious person by necessity and nature, he decided to walk along the ditch between the highway and the railroad tracks to look for pop bottles, which could be redeemed for a penny each. There were no bottles. Instead he found Luke—not that he was any more valuable than a bottle. Indeed, this find was actually a loss if you looked at it from a financial point of view.

But there he was, this microcosmic speck of humanity, knowing only his first name: Luke. (He adopted the name Satchell from Ophelia's family.) At that time, Luke didn't realize that people had more than one name. He did know that he lived in a shack close to a railroad freight yard, that his mother had died the previous winter, and a week or so ago his father had made his last appearance at their home.

Luke had been searching around an open-doored freight car for something to eat when he fell asleep and awoke to see the world going quickly past. The train had stopped on occasion, but he was afraid to disembark into strange surroundings. He just looked and looked at the changing scene, fully expecting his familiar home surroundings to reappear.

It was on the following day, when the train stopped at the siding near the strawberry auction block to load and unload, that his presence was discovered, and Luke's migration came to a halt. He was kicked off the freight car into a ditch, and that's where Nathan found him, scared and hungry—nothing new for him except the geographical location of his misery.

Nathan didn't want him (he would rather have found a pop bottle), but he knew that it would not be proper to leave him. Finally, after he had the chance to sell his now withered strawberries, Nathan put Luke into his cart and took him home.

Luke was different from the beginning. And, in rural Virginia in the twenties, to be different could be dangerous. His accent was peculiar, and he had to be kicked many times before he learned to always add a "Suh" to all affirmatives, negatives and almost any utterance when communicating with his inbred white superiors. He gradually learned, never understood, and always resented.

This was his new home, however, and even though he was shuffled from one family to another, it was probable that he was, at least for a while, better off than he had ever been.

Eventually, Luke and Ophelia decided to marry. I could say they fell in love, but most white folks in those days did not understand that such a romantic notion was possible with the poor blacks, especially those down in Hack's Neck.

After paying a dollar to a tent-meeting evangelist who claimed to have married them, Luke and Ophelia purchased a used cookstove and a crippled pig and moved into a one-room shack on a worn-out farm owned by an inbred white named George Trader. The farm was not far from Ophelia's parents' home. The arrangement, standard for the time, was that they would both have to work most of their time for Trader and would be paid a few pennies per hour for their toils.

Ophelia did this without resistance and never gave her "master" any trouble. However, Luke always reasoned that he was underpaid, and this led to a conflict between him and his employer/landlord. I'm not a psychologist, so I cannot say with authority if Luke's early northern environment affected his 'uppity' attitude. Perhaps it was his getting kicked off the train. Perhaps it was the beatings his superiors gave him when he forgot the "Suh". However, his rebellious attitude was evident throughout his short life.

It all came to an end in the summer of '29. This was a particularly bad year for farmers. First, there was too much rain in the spring, and the potatoes rotted in the ground and had to be replanted. Then there was not enough rain, and the potatoes and corn didn't get the moisture needed at the crucial time. But worst of all were the potato bugs. Certain vague, unfathomable conditions came together at the right time in the right proportions to cause a plague of these yellow and black beetles. In those days there were few chemical controls, and the crops had to be defended by hand-to-hand combat.

Ophelia and Luke were enlisted to squash bugs for Trader and, when time allowed, their own bugs on their little two-acre subsistence plot. Ophelia did her duty, but Trader wasn't pleased with Luke's efforts and decided to not pay him by the hour, but by the bug. This way he could be certain he was not being cheated. And it was an obsession with him to avoid being done unto by others as he would do unto them if he got the chance. A sort of unilateral agreement was made in which Luke would not squash the potato bugs but put them in yeast bottles. He was supposed to get a nickel per bottle, and Luke understood he would be paid this bounty upon delivery.

Luke worked two days to fill about a dozen bottles and took them to Trader only to be told to come back later for his pay. This infuriated Luke, who tried to convince Trader to pay as agreed. I think one would call it arguing, but Trader would hear none of it and decided to administer a "fine" for the back talk. He informed his jilted laborer that he wasn't going to be paid at all. Self-righteous Luke then reasoned that there was no alternative but to turn the bugs loose. He went back to the potato patch and shook the bottles empty. Trader saw this and went to the field and told Luke to move out of the shack that day. When Trader turned to leave, Luke, forgetting his humble pedigree once again, threw a yeast bottle at the back of his landlord's head and scored a direct hit. Trader did not even turn around but headed for the country store where a group of his colleagues were likely to be found sitting on the steps whittling.

It didn't take long. An hour later Luke was hanging from a sycamore tree in the church yard and Ophelia was a widow.

There was some sort of investigation. It did not occur immediately because the sheriff was an avid fisherman, and there was a big run of channel bass on at the time. But eventually he got down to Hack's Neck to look into this

insignificant matter. The body was gone by then. It disappeared the night after the lynching, and no one ever found it. Some suspect that Ophelia had it secretly buried. The noose was left dangling from a limb as a reminder, and years later I remember my father pointing out a piece of rope hanging from a tree—somewhere. I'm not sure it was the same one, but I hope it was.

The sheriff did ask a few questions, but no one seemed to know anything. Everyone in the area was related in some manner: a half-brother, cousin, uncle, full-sister or, usually, an assortment. Except for the inherent differences in gender or age, they all looked alike, talked alike and thought alike. "It was just like talking to the same person over and over," the sheriff said in an amused way. That was the end of that.

There is now a beautiful stained glass window in this church beside the hanging tree with George Trader's name leaded into it, commemorating this gentleman. It makes one fill up inside and choke a little to see it and read the engraving. You can go read it; I don't have space for it here. But there is nothing anywhere to note the quick and pathetic passing of Luke.

A few years ago, one of the Hack's Neck come-heres was having a septic system installed and a skeleton was uncovered from a shallow grave. It was an odd thing to see. Being obviously human and no different from anybody else's skeleton, including Trader's inbred frame, the remains initially attracted little attention—many poor folks in the old days took care of their own mortuary needs.

However, closer inspection revealed that the neck was broken, and along with a few threads of cloth and buttons were four or five yeast bottles. This did attract some musing before it was covered up, a marker placed and the septic system rerouted—a token of belated respect.

Soon after the lynching, Ophelia was also forced out of her home and was taken in by an old midwife, also a widow, who taught the young widow her trade. In later years she began to get into "sitting" and practical nursing as government programs and laws severely restricted midwifery.

Thus it was because of the potato bugs of 1929 that Mr. Rockwell received his long-needed enema and I met Aunt Ophelia. Or maybe it all came about because Ophelia's father looked for pop bottles in the ditch. That's the way life is: the drama of the present is molded by one of the infinite possible combinations of the tragedies and comedies of the past.

FOLLY'S LAST DAY

He was the best dog in the world,
and I am sure every reader has had one as good or better.

On the eastward side of the Chesapeake Bay, starting in Maryland and running south into Virginia, is a series of saltwater marshes. These marshes are separated from each other by tidal inlets, which cut into the peninsula at intervals, forming "necks" or mini-peninsulas.

These unique wetlands gradually diminish toward the south until, about thirty miles from Cape Charles at the mouth of the Bay, they disappear. The southernmost marsh of any size is bordered on the north by Nandua Creek and the south by Craddock Creek. These saltwater inlets penetrate the mainland in an easterly direction for about three miles, forming Craddock Neck.

The 1,200 acre tract bordering the Bay, which I will describe, is known locally as the "bottom" of Craddock Neck. This parcel has had various names corresponding to its owner: first Teakle Marsh in the 17th century, then Hyslop Marsh, and, to most local people today, Melson's

231

Marsh. It is surrounded on three sides by water and, depending on how you measure the guts and inlets, has ten to twelve miles of shoreline of diverse nature.

Starting on the sandy bay shore about three miles in length, there is a series of dunes six to eight feet high. They are not wide, 100 feet or so, and they fall off eastward to a terrain of myrtle, panic grass, beach persimmons and a few pines and cedars. In my youth there were clumps of huge loblolly pines on the bay shore, never timbered because of their remoteness. My friends and I would often rest in their shade after chasing horseshoe crabs and minnows and frolicking about in the unlittered shallows. We played just as Indian children had for thousands of years—I know this because in nature all children are the same. And I know Indians were there because of the middens, charcoal traces and arrowheads.

Now the trees are gone and all that remains are a few massive roots, far offshore, which will occasionally snag a fish net and jog the memory about better times. The shores are littered with plastic of every conceivable shape and color and the horseshoe crabs do not come here anymore.

The lower sand behind the dunes varies in its breadth of a few feet to several hundred before the ponds and the marsh begin. The ponds closer to the Bay are generally larger, some a few acres, and farther back into the marsh they are more numerous, but much smaller—mere potholes. Each of these small ponds is the private pool of a rail, a heron, or a black mallard, almost hidden by thick walls of black needlegrass.

In some slightly higher areas salt-meadow hay is the predominant vegetation and semi-wild cattle once foraged upon it. Mixed in this 700 acres of marsh are small clumps of ancient but stunted pine trees and myrtle bushes, sometimes called hummocks.

The marsh gradually fades into a thick forest of loblolly pines and occasional hollies as the land continues its imperceptible rise.

This almost virgin wilderness, if there is such a thing, belongs to me now, and it is here, where wetland meets forest, that I have a special place where I sometimes come to think and sometimes to not think, depending on the dictates of moods and happenings—but always to observe. Here, soon after the acquisition of this property, I built a small tree house supported by four of the larger loblolly pines overlooking the area.

It is a simple affair, a four foot by four foot by six foot box with a lid. There is some discarded carpet on the floor for comfort and a small peep hole on each side. Its sole furnishings are a pen and writing pad and a bushel basket for a seat. My vantage point is only about 25 feet high, but with binoculars the view is always spectacular, and never the same. The infinite combination of season, weather, time of day and the whims of the actors that trod this stage assure one of a constantly changing drama.

It is a brief walk from Corratock, the land's main 1780 dwelling, through pines and hollies before one reaches this

233

pristine spot. I come here all seasons for all reasons. Often I pretend to be a deer hunter, but in reality I am only a looker, even though I have a gun. I seek a world record buck, and say to myself and others that I would try to kill it. I might try but hope, of course, to fail and hope further there will not be the chance.

In my earlier years I was an avid and successful hunter. I was, in those formative times, driven by an instinct instilled in me by all my preceding generations, when all men were hunters. Now, after decades of interpreting birds, animals and humans in bronze sculpture, I have come to revere life. I find it difficult to kill.

On this special fall day about which I will tell, I came here to escape. Folly, my border collie, a devoted companion of sixteen years, was sick. I sat in my tree house in the loblolly pines overlooking the marsh and the distant Bay, thinking of the day my son brought him home on a weekend trip from college to be adopted by the Turners. As I inspected the ten-dollar dog, which for some reason did not have papers, I did not realize the reciprocal of this adoption was true. How could I know this black and white bundle with a worm-swollen belly (having just soiled the kitchen floor) was a living treasure and would always be with me or waiting for me.

In the ensuing days after his arrival, this creature began to follow me everywhere I went, if he could keep up. He received no special treatment from me but soon became a boon companion. He was the best dog in the world, and I am sure every reader has had one as good or better. That's the way it is with men and dogs.

Memories followed memories as I looked out over the land that Folly and I had trod together over the years.

As two o'clock approached, the time that the veterinarian would come, I knew that if I abandoned my perch in the trees and ran through the woods to Corratock to make the telephone call, I could spare him for a few days. But to what purpose? Folly deserved an impartial judgment and I knew mine would be selfish—wanting to keep him beyond his time. He did not need to continue to suffer, to endure the humiliation of defecating on himself or of having to be lifted to the seat of my truck where he loved to ride. What he needed, I knew, was a little prodding to quit hanging on.

This day he could not stand without help and my employee, Kathy, who loves all dogs, especially Folly, said he would not eat. But I offered him some morsels of hamburger and he ate. I said goodbye to him at noon and, as we looked at each other for the last time, I was convinced that he knew and understood—he was a smart dog. Nevertheless, I left instructions to save Folly if he could be made comfortable and that neither expense nor trouble should enter into this live-or-die decision. This offered hope, something we all need no matter how minuscule it is.

When I left him, he was panting continuously, and I suppose the inoperable tumor on his lung was not allowing enough life-giving oxygen. Of all deaths, I imagine that suffocation is the least desirable. The body has evolved so that a signal is given when it needs water, food or oxygen, and it is the need of the last that has the most urgency.

One thought breeds another and I recall a legend that came with Corratock. It has been handed down that in the late 17th century, before the original house was burned by the British, the mistress of the land was feeding her fowl in the barnyard when she was attacked and bitten by a rabid fox and became ill. Rabies, too, is a horribly painful death and, of course, in those times it was incurable. As her agony intensified, her husband mercifully directed the servants to place a pillow over her face. So it was done until her struggles ceased. It would seem that a musket ball would have been less painful, but there must have been some aversion to blood and noise.

At quarter after two, normally a quiet time, a great horned owl began to hoot, interrupting my thoughts. I had never heard one so early, so loud or so close. I was sure of being told by some unknown entity that Folly was dead. But this signal was so clear, it scared me. We do not

236

know about all that is out there—not the scientists, not the preachers and certainly not me.

The owl called prematurely, and a kingfisher rattled out its cry as it changed vantage points in its continuous quest for minnows. The large bird of darkness never emits its soft "whoo" while in flight. The small kingfisher, on the other hand, is abroad in daylight, and when its sharp call is heard, one knows that it is in flight. The muted browns and black of the owl contrast with the steel blue and white of the kingfisher. And one should note in this time of feminism that the female owl is larger than the male, and the female kingfisher, with a splash of rust on its breast, is the only bird in North America more colorful than its male counterpart. Although the ultimate goal of all of Nature's planning is survival, this is sometimes achieved with opposite designs.

Two young grey squirrels, probably siblings, chased each other in a large myrtle bordering the woods. One jumped to an adjoining tree, clasped a small branch with its front paws, climbed to the pinnacle and mocked its companion. After some hesitation, the latter made a leap for the same branch but, because of some inherent deficiency in its judgment or strength, could not bridge the gap and fell a dozen feet to the ground—no problem for an arboreal rodent with a fluffy tail.

But this comedy was soon followed by tragedy when a Cooper's Hawk dived through some thick myrtle bushes and came to rest on a rotten pine limb with a male cardinal in its claws. It began to tear into the flesh with its beak even before the puff of red feathers had fluttered to the marsh. Success for the predator and failure for the prey—nature's continuing cycle of life and death.

In the Bay, gannets dove like a shower of white arrows into a school of fish. A few brown pelicans that would soon go south cautiously fished the fringes of the school, as if their fellow fishermen were too dangerous with their repeated plunging.

A flock of green-winged teal approached closely, circled, looked for a safe haven and finally landed on a pond partially created by a ditch made centuries ago in an effort to drain this marsh, when it was higher and had more potential for grazing cattle. Suddenly they took flight, apparently frightened by a danger too subtle for me to detect. They flew off in one direction and I watched them leave. As they hastily departed, I saw a lone duck flying in the opposite direction. I assumed first that it had just decided for no reason to take an opposing course. But it was so frantic in its flight that I sensed there was something different transpiring on my stage. And there was—a peregrine falcon was about twenty yards behind, closing

fast. The pursued and the pursuer flew into the pine woods and disappeared from view. I did not see the small duck again, but in a few moments the frustrated peregrine appeared, flying slower and conserving its energy for another attempt. The teal knew there was a chance in the trees, and it lived.

Over Back Creek, an immature bald eagle worked hard on the day shift, circling and watching for its prey, a duck or a rail. He may have to scavenge for a fish washed upon the shore if he is not successful in his hunt. Failures occur, and we all settle for less when necessary.

It was beginning to rain and the breeze strengthened and skimmed across the vast acreage of needlegrass, creating an undulating brown sea with eddies of turbulence in the shorter and softer salt-meadow hay. Small, swaying islands of pine periodically break this monotony of grass and, although stunted and small, are old beyond their appearance.

As dusk approached, a yearling deer crossed the stream in front of my treetop hiding place and came past my blind. Sensing my presence by sound or smell or sight, or some of each, it nervously twitched its tail and hurried into the thicker woods. Its mother browsed some distance behind and, oblivious to the danger sensed by her offspring, moved ahead in the same path. Suddenly, she stopped where her fawn had, raised a front foot and listened and looked, testing the air in my direction. In a decisive manner she stomped the soft mud and then turned and re-crossed the stream. On the far side she paused and looked back for her fawn. After several minutes she called a short one-syllable cry—a raspy plaintive beckoning. Every few minutes this was repeated from a slightly different vantage point, each from the safety of cover but always directed at the point of separation. The novice eventually responded and joined its wiser parent.

Dusk is prime time on the marsh. There is an invariable increase in vocal and physical activity at the time when day gives way to night. The rails (clapper, Virginia, black and sora) as well as the owls (great horned and barred) voice their recognition of the change from light to darkness, as these and other creatures exercise their primordial instincts.

Ducks will settle into the ponds along the bay shore for food, drink and sleep. It is a good time to observe or kill, hear or think, and I remain in my tree top blind until I absorb every last drop of golden pleasure from the panoramic view, deluged with an intriguing narrative and a pleasant serenade.

A heavily muscled buck of eight points emerged from the thick pine woods. He was on a well-trodden route that leads to a lush green field of clover about a half-mile away. The monarch paused at the edge of the woods where myrtles bordered the marsh. He looked, listened and smelled in all directions as a child might at an unfamiliar school crossing, then stepped forth into the full force of the rain and wind. It was blowing vehemently now as the light faded, and the rain had begun to sting my face. The pines swayed with incessant gusts of wind and so did my tree house. The buck made a few steps into the unsheltered marsh and hesitated. He was clearly uncomfortable with the inclement weather which was inhibiting his ability to detect danger. Then, slowly and in a determined way, he returned to the shelter of the woods and disappeared. He would not dine in the clover field that night.

The sun was setting across the Chesapeake, and under the gray rain clouds the long and narrow Back Creek was a reddish-orange dancing runway leading into its source—a half-submerged and homogeneous ball of fire. The light was ebbing with the tide, and owls now called from all directions. The intervals of their hoots indicated they were communicating to each other, albeit in a primitive manner. There were two distinctive calls, but I cannot attribute the difference between these sounds to mood, sex, or any other factor. The Virginia rail, a little smaller than the more numerous clapper rail, joined the chorus and cackled frequently, reminding me of my grandfather cranking his Model T.

Every once in a while great blue herons squawked with startlement as they were disturbed at their private fishing ponds by deer or raccoon. The herons only call when alarmed or fighting with their own kind.

In the distance, large ducks, probably black mallards, settled into the small brackish ponds that lie behind the low sand dunes next to the Bay. They would spend the night there, sheltered from the relentless waves of the Chesapeake. If the tide was low, many would find shelter in the shallow water between the exposed sand bars.

It was now cold, windy and semi-dark, and I reluctantly began my return to the warm fireside of Corratock. On this moonlit evening in November, as I was finding my way home past a tidal inlet, I was told to pause in this place for something special. Perhaps it was the bright moonlight peeking through the clouds and glimmering on the surface of the salt water in a thousand minute strobes that told me this. Or maybe my old bones just needed a rest.

As I looked out over the surface of the water between the pines, I first sensed then realized the presence of something unusual. On the water's surface were two protrusions. Each was about two feet long, six or eight inches high and tapered fore and aft to nothing. As I looked at these objects, I detected that they were moving very slowly at exactly the same rate of speed, yet they made no wake, no disturbance, and thus obviously were not self-propelled. Their symmetry, their synchronous movement and their shape suggested that these objects were alive. I realized they were being slowly propelled by the wind. And because there were two, not three and not one, this indicated some bond. Dinosaurs, muskrats, turtles and raccoons were considered and rejected. Finally, by the time-honored method of elimination, I was left with the only possibility—otters.

Yet they were not otters as we normally see them—playing, swimming and frolicking. They had something else programmed into them this evening as they disappeared into the black needle grass.

Back at Corratock, I learned the bad news, possibly for

243

the second time that day—Folly was gone.   David, my middle son, had already buried him in the woods he loved to roam.

Not even man, in his ruthless destruction of himself and his environment, can match nature when she decides to destroy. But in a different mood she is an unequaled healer, and I had been given a dose of her tonic.

It is a bit of trouble to weave a net, hang it in, then immerse it into the depths of the Bay. However, once this is done, there is a period of satisfaction and expectation while one lies awake at night wondering what has been gilled. So it is with writing and drawing a book. Will you be ignored as the public swims in another direction or will readers become entangled so numerously that their tails are overlapping?

As a boy, I built boats with boards, then birds, animals and humans with clay. But there is no challenge as great as building a book, and there is a permanence to the written word that exceeds timber or metal. The only limits are one's life experience—and imagination.

245